AUGUSTUS HARE
IN ITALY

AUGUSTUS HARE
IN ITALY

Edited by Gavin Henderson
from the Italian travel books of Augustus Hare
and illustrated from the original
wood engravings

WITH AN INTRODUCTION BY
SACHEVERELL SITWELL

MICHAEL RUSSELL

First published in Great Britain 1977
in an edition of 850 copies
by Michael Russell (Publishing) Ltd.
The Chantry, Wilton, Salisbury
and designed and printed
by The Compton Press Ltd.
The Old Brewery, Tisbury, Wilts
Introduction © Sacheverell Sitwell 1977
Set in Monotype Centaur
ISBN 0 85955 046 X
All rights reserved

Publisher's Note

We should like to acknowledge – apart from his editorial assistance – the kindness of Mr. John Saumarez Smith in making available to us the collection of wood engravings originally used to illustrate Augustus Hare's Italian travel books. Not all had survived and the condition of others had suffered in varying degrees. (Indeed, there were five casualties in the final stages of production which have had to be replaced by line blocks.) Mr. Gavin Henderson's editorial objective has been to assemble a wide-ranging selection and match Hare's text to it. In doing so he has drawn on the following illustrated works (which do, of course, in some instances overlap one another): *Cities of Northern Italy*, vols. 1 & 2; *The Rivieras*; *Venice* (5th edition, 1900); *Florence* (3rd edition, 1890); *Cities of Central Italy*, vols. 1 & 2; *Days Near Rome*, vols. 1 & 2; *Cities of Southern Italy and Sicily*. (The celebrated two-volume *Walks in Rome* was not illustrated.)

The index map is by Denys R. Baker.

Contents & List of Illustrations

Introduction

I T IS in the nature of a happy coincidence for me that Augustus Hare's entry into Italy at the start of this anthology should be in the region of San Remo. For that is where I had my own first experience of Italy at five or six years old, and I am not going to forget it. At the mere mention of the name I see again the palm trees of the Corso, the golden domes of the Russian Church, and the railway line running in silly fashion along the tideless seashore as though specially to please me, for my delight in those days lay in counting the railway trucks as they rolled by. Or else, in a diversion of a different kind, I suddenly hear again the screech and blare of the bicycle band of the *Bersagliere*, tearing through the streets in their feathered hats, blowing their trumpets happily and furiously as they rush past.

My parents had taken a villa for the winter with the first painted ceilings I had ever seen. For sheer *joie de vivre* there were even simulated telegraph wires in paint along the cornices. (Many years later in Malta I was to be reminded of this by a drawing-room ceiling where along the frieze, in sign of *art nouveau*, a pair of cupids in stucco were telephoning each other, and the telephones were formed of stucco roses.) We had made friends, young and old, and had met Russian and Polish and Austrian families living in the villas and hotels. The San Remo of thirty years before, when Augustus Hare was writing of it, cannot have been so very different. In the main it was a British and a Russian expatriate colony, with two Anglican churches and as many as five 'resident British physicians' even as late as my Baedeker of 1913.

And I remove from San Remo by recounting how, thirty years later, in 1938, 'grown up' by then and married, we arrived in the dead of night at Cracow on our way to stay at the most famous of Polish country houses, to be told in the morning that a Polish gentleman living in the hotel wished us to come up and see him. He was the survivor of two brothers I remembered all those years before in San Remo – delicate-looking young men who used to come to dinner and play bridge, charmed I think a little by my mother's good looks. The following day he invited us to see his head peasants from the Tatra mountains, who had come in to pay their rents and who were wearing splendid embroidered white peasant's costumes and had eagles' feathers in their wide-brimmed hats. A divagation, I know, but how it would have interested and amused Augustus.

So we are off along the coast by carriage, and now and then by train. 'Sketching' is an important consideration, and it is noticeable how often Augustus mentions 'artistic subjects for the pencil'. Almost at the outset of our journey he is inviting us to try 'some of the narrow alleys, where artists will find charming subjects of the older palms feathering over little shrines or bridges'. But we are not to be misled and taken in by first impressions. Even allowing for the unavoidable sex change, this is not in the least 'the bland, shy sketching person' of Henry James's tale 'The Third Person', 'whom fate had condemned to a monotony – triumphing over variety – of Swiss and Italian *pensions*; in any of which with well-fastened hat, stout boots, camp-stool, sketch book and Tauchnitz novel, "he" would have served with peculiar propriety as a frontispiece to the natural history of the English old maid.' Any more in fact than Henry James himself. And yet 'old maid', yes, in many respects. Fussy, easily shocked, though delighting in it; with secret, or hidden, side to him; but a person of formidable learning and acuity, a huge, inexhaustible store of historical knowledge, and an extraordinary repository, as well, of spine-chilling anecdote and story.

At the moment it is the picturesque and mediaeval that Augustus is in search of along the Ligurian coast, and if there is anything of the sort he will hunt it out and try both to describe and draw it. A little sadly, since there is not room for everything, we are whirled away before he has time to tell us of the Cinque Terre district that I am sure he would have loved: five villages forming a kind of independent mediaeval wine co-operative of their own, with the vines trained upon wires across the gorges and up the cliffs, and only to be reached by ladders or even from a boat. For all these endurances the wine itself, which I have tasted, is a disappointment.

But certainly there is no monotony of narrative with Genoa, Turin and Milan following in quick succession. By now we are becoming confirmed admirers of the woodcut vignettes and are scrambling with the author-artist round some of the little paths below the Madonna del Sasso to a point 'well known to our water-colour artists'. How old-fashioned that sounds! Augustus is endearing in his affection for old monasteries and convents, and he loved to draw them. He is not remembered as a draughtsman, but these vignettes from his sketches form a most remarkable appendix to the great body of Victorian woodcuts. They could perhaps be set beside the earlier steel-engraved vignettes after Turner, who in general is more interested in clouds and sky and distance than in buildings. For a good example of Augustus Hare at his best, look at his view of the Arno at Pisa with the little prickly chapel of the Madonna della Spina on the riverbank, with the wood-engraver's name, W. M. R. Quick, lying in the foreground shallows. This is an artistic partnership of more than considerable achievement.

That Augustus's ideas of the 'picturesque' are a little trite is already obvious. But at the time he was at work rather more than a hundred years ago, disrepair, ever and always an important element in the 'picturesque', had hardly begun to affect buildings of the seventeenth and eighteenth centuries, which because of that, if for little other reason, had no interest or appeal for him. It was then due to this slow 'creep forward' and advance in time that writers of my own generation found themselves drawn to the romantic dilapidation of buildings in Naples, in Apulia and Sicily, and to the correlative architecture in Portugal and Spain. What Augustus Hare would have said and written if faced with the gaieties and exuberance of Rococo abbeys and churches in Bavaria I do not like to think. Yet, if born in a later generation, there is little doubt that his opinions would have altered accordingly. In fact, what the writer needs, no less than the composer, is a good libretto; and all of this in theory and in practice is subject to the laws of time. We are no longer in the age when 'artists will find beautiful subjects in the ascent behind the town, looking towards Genoa'; while in comical antithesis we are conjecturing whatever Donizetti, composer of a Romantic masterpiece, *Lucia di Lammermoor*, and of the Italian *commedia Don Pasquale*, can have had in mind when writing his early *opera semiseria, l' Eremitaggio di Liverpool?* What indeed? And it is too late now to know.

We arrive now at 'the promontory, where Byron wrote his *Corsair* upon the cliffs', thinking in rapid thought transference of the *Corsaire* overture of Berlioz, of Byronic inspiration presumably; and of poor Berlioz returning half-dead from his giant concerts in Moscow and St. Petersburg in the winter months of 1868-9, travelling three days and four nights in the train, bound for Nice in order to fulfil his wish 'to be bathed in violets and sleep in the sun'. For although Augustus Hare rejoiced in that sort of landscape, we cannot see him wanting to be bathed in violets or even attempting a siesta in the shade. And incidentally he seems to have been totally impervious to music. How 'old maid' Augustus and Hector Berlioz would have disliked each other!

'Here we must leave our carriage, and engage horses for the ascent to La Vernia', an ascent I would have loved to have undertaken with Augustus. And hence in a fleeting moment to the monastery of Monte Oliveto Maggiore where some indication of the landscape is given, but without reference to its rocky and eremitic wildness, and with no mention of the more than wonderful frescoes by Signorelli, which seem to be based on studies of the Teutonic *landsknects* then wandering round and murdering all over Central Italy. Great play is made by Signorelli of the flashing lights and varying colours on their armour.

And so on to Ravenna and to Rimini. We are not to think

that Augustus Hare was oblivious to the mosaics in San Vitale, or to the sculptural perfections of the Tempio Malatestiana at Rimini, these two being indeed among the wonders of the Western world. They are not illustrated here for they are not 'subjects' for his pencil, but in his text he gives long and most careful descriptions and historical accounts of them. And hence to Gubbio, still mercifully eight miles from a railway though loud with motors, even now one of the least spoilt of Italian towns, its population only five times more than a hundred years ago instead of the usual eight or nine.

By now there are quite a few instances of how tastes differ within a generation or two, or even less than that. 'The vast cathedral', for instance, 'of Orvieto, with its delicate spray-like pinnacles, and its golden and jewelled front.' It is now more than half a century since I first saw it and disliked it, as, too, the cathedral of Siena, both inside and out – and the passage of time only confirms me in my first impression. This is not the real and true *métier* of the Italians; Gothic is essentially of the north, and not for the light and sun of Italy. But the old and true Italy of the past emerges in Hare's account of market day in Perugia, with 'goats and oxen and flocks of sheep, attended by their gaily dressed herdsmen, who sing wild *stornelli* in deep Umbrian voices as they go.' We are back in Childe Harold's Italy to the music again of Berlioz, of whom we may be thinking hereabouts when reading of 'a fortress for the imprisonment of brigands'; and if we substitute kidnapper for brigand it becomes the eternal Italy of legend and probably all time.

It has already been observed that Augustus had no ear for music. Not for him to sing for us, or play the cello after dinner. And it could be worse than that on mid-Victorian evenings. An old lady I know told me that her mother when going to stay for Christmas with a rich relation in Shropshire used to bring her harp with her which travelled in the guard's van. Instead of anything of that sort, Augustus would be telling us ghost stories, a talent for which he had almost international fame. Witness his *Autobiography*, in an astonishing six volumes. It is one of the most curiously enjoyable works of the Victorian age, full of nearly incredible stories; the mechanical lady who propelled herself along, but I cannot remember now if the machinery was noiseless or not; the serpentine daughter of the Swedish countess who glided across the passage into Augustus's mother's sitting room, entirely naked, moving on her stomach with head raised and eyes shut, passing in and out between the legs of a table or two, then back again to the countess, who, when questioned about it by the 'mother' of Augustus (she was his stepmother), would only remark 'Yes, it happens sometimes' and would say no more. Or the story of the 'elemental', which I remember being criticized by an 'authority' on such subjects who wrote that not only was the story impossible to credit but the persons involved were unidentifiable. Yet, with only slight research they emerged as the family of the not exactly beloved headmaster of my penitentiary private school.

The six volumes, for those with the time for it in their lives, cannot be too warmly recommended, together with Nancy Mitford's understanding and amusing essay on Augustus to go with them. And indeed a thorough reading of his works would occupy some months on end. His *Paris* and *Days near Paris,* his books on Russia and on Spain, are brimming with anecdote and information, not to be found elsewhere. While his four volumes on provincial France, North-East, South-West, and so on, still amount almost to a *terra incognita* for most readers, and are as readable as when they appeared some eighty to ninety years ago.

Perhaps where his books on Italy are concerned Augustus Hare is at his most congenial in *Cities of Southern Italy and Sicily*. Or is it only I am waiting to see what he has to say of those places which had such a fascination for me when I was in my twenties? For the sake of harmonious relations it is probably safer to avoid controversial 'subjects', even 'for the pencil', and agree on what is common ground between us.

Amalfi for an instance 'where only man is vile', and where he complains of 'the dreadful pest of beggars which has grown up under the Sardinian government'; but he would hate it even more today with all the beach umbrellas and the bus-loads on package tours. And of a sudden I am made to feel old at his mention of the Hotel Cappuccini and its proprietor and landlord Don Matteo Vozzi, because I remember so well his son Don Alfredo, and the five or six winters spent there all those years ago trying to become a writer:

'But ever impatient,
How much I longed already
    to transcend and surpass the landscape,
And reach to places outside and beyond
    the ordinary pale of writing and of poetry,
Anticipating years of travel to far off and exotic lands;
On a morning of frost upon the black-green leaves
    and lit lanterns of the tangerines: –
Dreaming often of the temples of Angkor,
And from my window at Amalfi
    looking across the sea to Spain.'

I have strong feelings about Amalfi still, and about beautiful Ravello lying up above it through the lemon and orange groves, and cannot express myself upon it in any other medium than verse. And who knows? Maybe Augustus Hare would agree with me.

We have reached the end of his illustrated travels. But we have another visit to describe: we will invite Augustus to Montegufoni, for a long time our family home in Tuscany. In order to effect the transformation some sleight of hand is necessary – some degree of scene-shifting, of putting back of clocks and advancing of others, of altering of ages. My brother, it is true, remembered Augustus being brought over to Renishaw from another country house in 1903 or 4, just about the time of our opening chapter at San Remo. But he was a boy of ten or eleven and only recalled the fact of it and none of the details. Augustus would then have been seventy or thereabouts. So we will leave him at that, while 'back-dating' ourselves so that I am twenty-five years old, the age of promise with unfulfilment still ahead; my brother thirty, and my sister thirty-five. My father who has long been an admirer of his writings is particularly anxious to meet him. I myself am enthusiastic, if a little nervous, but his name means less than nothing to my sister and my mother. And so the invitation has been issued and accepted. I confess I am looking forward with a good deal of nervous trepidation to tomorrow's visit, made worse by my having brought it on myself. He is to drive out here and we are to expect him early in the evening.

Augustus has come and gone. And I would describe it as an enjoyable evening, but not one that I would like to have repeated over and over again. He looks frail and old; and when asked 'last thing' what he wanted in the morning requested 'a lightly boiled egg and a shawl at half-past seven'. It was not too bad in the early part of the evening. Augustus had stopped on the way here, as I expected he would, to revisit the tombs of the Acciaiuoli, the family who built and owned the castle, at the Certosa just outside Florence. And this gave something to talk about. Of course he was interested in the older part of the house, and in particular the cortile, only just cleared; for it had been filled up with a warren of rooms, where was found still hanging in place the azure-painted shield with its carved stone lilies of the Prince of Taranto, son of Queen Joanna of Naples, who had taken refuge here in 1348 with Niccolo Acciaiuoli, Grand Seneschal of the Kingdom, bringing Boccaccio with him, and fleeing perhaps as much from the plague as from his enemies. And so on, until it became more than a little boring. And then my father began on mediaeval choral dancing, a favourite conversational gambit of his, and embarked on with the enthusiasm of a young boy or girl discussing, say, a performance of the latest musical. Then conversation languished; but soon after, more as though we were fatiguing him, which was probably the truth, just after nine o'clock he withdrew upstairs to bed. And we were alone with Augustus which had its awkward silences. I think he had a distaste for persons younger than himself, and would have cordially disliked my sister's poems, had it been possible in time for him to read them.

The member of the family he liked most would have been my father who had at least travelled exhaustively in Southern Italy, indeed to fastnesses that Augustus Hare had never reached. But he was too self-opinionated. At least, though, he had had the boldness and temerity to buy this huge old half-ruined castle and try to live in it; so unlike Augustus the peripatetic, always on the move, and equipped for it with special devices for ridding his room at the inn of insect pests, protecting himself against damp sheets or catching colds, and so forth. And, from my father's point of view, Augustus knew too many people. 'Such a mistake to have friends' was a favourite maxim with him, while Augustus would prattle by the hour about old ladies who were his cronies.

So they were temperamentally unsuited, the one real link between them being the religious maniac background of both their childhoods, although they belonged in fact to different generations. My brother and sister I do not think he understood at all and he expressed an ill-concealed horror at my telling him I was trying to write of the baroque in Italy and Sicily. And yet as *Inglese Italianato* there was not all that difference between Augustus and at least the male members of my family. And as he drove away to Florence in the morning I was remembering, as I am doing now, the booking-clerk in Thomas Cook and Son who when asked once too often by the hundredth old American or English lady how to get from Florence to Siena, yelled 'Change at Empoli and Poggibonsi', slapping each side of her face as he did so. He was given the sack in consequence, but soon reinstated by popular appeal to which we signed our names. And that was the old Italy of Augustus Hare.

SACHEVERELL SITWELL

Dolceacqua

FTER TWO miles more, winding through woods of olives, carpeted in spring by young corn and bright green flax, Dolceacqua suddenly bursts upon the view, stretching across a valley, whose sides are covered with forests of olives and chestnuts, and which is backed by fine snow mountains. Through the town winds the deep-blue stream of the Nervia, flowing under a tall bridge of one wide arch, and above frowns the huge palatial castle, perched upon a perpendicular cliff, with sunlight streaming through its long lines of glassless windows. The streets are almost closed in with archways, which give them the look of gloomy crypts, only opening here and there to let in a ray of sunlight and a strip of blue sky. They lead up the steep ascent to the castle where the Doria once reigned as sovereign princes, as the Grimaldi at Monaco.

Bordighera, which has been surnamed 'the Jericho of Italy', was almost unknown in England a few years ago, but is now familiar through Signor Ruffini's beautiful story of *Doctor Antonio*, of which the principal scene is laid here. The town contains nothing worth visiting, so that it is best to leave the carriage in the street, and wander up the hill, first to the garden of the French consul, where are some of the finest palm trees; then up some of the narrow alleys, where artists

23

At Bordighera

will find charming subjects of the older palms feathering over little shrines or bridges; and then to the common on the hill-top, with its grand view to Mentone, Roccabruna, and Monaco, and in the vaporous distance, to Antibes and the faint blue mountains of Provence. A winding path descends from the heights to the shore at the point of the rocky bay, which is the scene of one of the word-pictures of Ruffini.

S. Remo is greatly changed within the last few years, and from a quiet fishing port has become a town of more than 18,000 inhabitants and one of the great southern centres for sun-seeking invalids; but in beauty it is greatly inferior to Mentone, and there are very few drives and walks.

To the quiet of charms and sunshine S. Remo adds that of a peculiar beauty. The Apennines rise like a screen behind the amphitheatre of soft hills that enclose it – hills soft with olive woods, and dipping down with gardens of lemon and orange, and vineyards, dotted with palms. An iso-lated space juts out from the centre of the semicircle, and from summit to base it tumbles the oddest of Italian towns, a strange mass of arches and churches and steep lanes, rushing down like a stone cataract to the sea. On either side of the town lie deep ravines, with lemon gardens along their bottoms, and olives thick along their sides. The olive is the characteristic tree of San Remo.

Saturday Review, January 1871

At S. Remo

Taggia itself is deep down in the valley by the side of the rushing river of the same name. Its streets are curious; several of its houses have been handsome *palazzi,* and there is still a native aristocracy resident in the place. Many of the old build-

Lampedusa from Taggia

Castellaro

ings are painted on the outside with fading frescoes; of others
the stone fronts are cut into diamond facets, others are richly
carved. Most of them rest upon open arches, in which are
shops where umbrella-vendors set out their bright wares, and
crimson *berrette* hang out for sale, enlivening the grey walls by
their brilliant colouring. All the spots described in the novel
of *Doctor Antonio* really exist, and the crowd which collects
around the carriage of strangers when it stops, invites them
to visit the house of 'Signora Eleanora', 'Il Baronetto Inglese',
etc. The long bridge across the valley is adorned with a shrine
commemorating the adventure of two children who were
thrown down by an earthquake with two of its arches in
1831, and escaped uninjured. From the other side of the
bridge, a path turning to the right mounts by a steep ascent
to the many-arched Castellaro, where the church stands out
finely on the spur of the hill, its tower relieved against the
blue background of the sea. It has been mostly rebuilt since
the earthquake of 1887.

Following the windings of the hill, a path leads hence
to Lampedusa.

A broad, smooth road, opening from Castellaro northwards, and
stretching over the side of the steep mountains in capricious zig-zags, now
conceals, now gives to view, the front of the sanctuary, shaded by two oaks
of enormous dimensions. The Castellini, who made this road 'in the sweat

of their brows', point it out with pride, and well they may. They tell you, with infinite complacency, how every one of the pebbles with which it is paved was brought from the sea-shore, those who had mules using them for that purpose, those who had none bringing up loads on their own backs; how every one, gentleman and peasant, young and old, women and boys, worked day and night, with no other inducement than the love of the Madonna. The Madonna of Lampedusa is their creed, their occupation, their pride, their *carroccio*, their fixed idea.

All that relates to the miraculous image, and the date and mode of its translation to Castellaro, is given at full length in two inscriptions, one in Latin, the other in bad Italian verses, which are to be seen in the interior of the little chapel of the sanctuary. Andrea Anfosso, a native of Castellaro, being the captain of a privateer, was one day attacked and defeated by the Turks, and carried to the Isle of Lampedusa. Here he succeeded in making his escape, and hiding himself until the Turkish vessel which had captured his left the island. Anfosso, being a man of expedients, set about building a boat, and finding himself in a great dilemma what to do for a sail, ventured on the bold and original step of taking from the altar of some church or chapel of the island a picture of the Madonna to serve as one; and so well did it answer his purpose, that he made a most prosperous voyage back to his native shores, and, in a fit of generosity, offered his holy sail to the worship of his fellow townsmen. The wonder of the affair does not stop here. A place was chosen by universal acclamation, two gunshots in advance of the present sanctuary, and a chapel erected, in which the gift was deposited with all due honour. But the Madonna, as it would seem,

La Madonna di Lampedusa

27

had an insurmountable objection to the spot selected, for, every morning that God made, the picture was found at the exact spot where the actual church now stands. Sentinels were posted at the door of the chapel, the entire village remained on foot for nights, mounting guard at the entrance; no precaution, however, availed. In spite of the strictest watch, the picture, now undeniably a miraculous one, found means to make its way to the spot preferred. At length, the Castellini came to understand that it was the Madonna's express wish that her headquarters should be shifted to where her resemblance betook itself every night; and though it had pleased her to make choice of the most abrupt and the steepest spot on the whole mountain, just where it was requisite to raise arches in order to lay a sure foundation for her sanctuary, the Castellini set themselves *con amore* to the task so clearly revealed to them, and this widely renowned chapel was completed. This took place in 1619. In the course of time some rooms were annexed for the accommodation of visitors and pilgrims, and a terrace built; for though the Castellini have but a small purse, theirs is the great lever which can remove all impediments – the faith that brought about the Crusades.

RUFFINI

Approach to Badalucco

Beyond Taggia the road winds through a magnificent mountain ravine to Badalucco (14 k.), an excursion well worth making. There is only room for the torrent Argentina and the road, through the depth of the valley: the lower

28

slopes of the hills are covered with fine old chestnut trees. At Badalucco, the river is crossed by a very lofty bridge supporting a chapel and a gateway.

Albenga (inn: Grand Hotel, new and good) is the ancient Albium Ingaunum and birthplace of the Emperor Proculus. Its thirteen mediaeval towers remind the Italian traveller of S. Gimignano, rising out of the plain like a number of tall ninepins set close together. Albenga affords many artistic subjects, possessing a very ancient Gothic cathedral, an early baptistery – green with mould and damp, and three equally grim and green Lombardic lions at the foot of the tower called Torre del Marchese Malespina. A little way beyond the town is a Roman bridge, Ponte Lungo. The place is so unhealthy that 'hai faccia di Albenga' is a proverbial expression in the country for one who looks ill.

Cathedral of Albenga

Savona (inn: Hotel Suisse, excellent) is the largest town on the coast after Nice and Genoa, and has a small but safe harbour. The handsome cathedral of 1604 contains, in the Cappella Sistina, the tomb of the parents of Pope Sixtus IV.

At Savona

In S. Giacomo is the tomb of the lyric poet Chiabrera, who was born here, inscribed by his own desire:

> 'Amico, io, vivendo, cercava conforto
> Nel Monte Parnasso;
> Tu, meglio consigliato, cercalo
> Nel Calvario.'

The house in which Chiabrera lived in the town is inscribed with the motto he chose – 'Nihil ex omni parte beatum.' The theatre is dedicated to Chiabrera. Pius VII was long detained at Savona as a prisoner. Artists will not fail to sketch the lovely view from the port with its old tower. The statue of the Virgin here has an inscription which can be read either in Latin or Italian:

> 'In mare irato, in subita procella,
> Invoco te, nostra benigna stella.'

       ✳   ✳   ✳

To the left of the cathedral square [in Genoa] by the Via and Salita del Arcivescovado, we reach the Church of S. Matteo. The story of the Doria family circles around this little building. It is supposed to have had its romantic origin in Arduin, Vicomte de Narbonne, who fell ill at Genoa when he came

30

thither to embark for the Crusades, and was kindly nursed by a noble Genoese lady of the Della Volta family, and her daughter Oria. This kindness Arduin never forgot, and, when he returned from the Holy Land, he married Oria, and merging his nationality into hers, and calling his property Port d'Oria, became the ancestor of the most illustrious family in Genoa. On the raised loggia before the church, the Doria merchants met their clients, and hence Andrea Doria harangued the people in 1528, urging them to resist the French, who were them besieging the town. The little piazza is surrounded by the family palaces.

In the beautiful little cloister, on the left of the church, are the remains of the colossal statues of Andrea and Giovandrea (son of Gianetto) Doria erected in front of the Doge's palace in 1577, and decapitated and mutilated by the mob in 1797.

Cloister of S. Matteo, Genoa

No. 5 of the Via Balbi is the Palazzo dell'Università, approached from its cortile by a magnificent staircase, guarded by the most grand lions. It contains some statues and bas-reliefs by Giovanni da Bologna, and has a museum of natural history and a botanical garden. On the steps is the tomb of Simone Boccanegra, the first and best of the Doges, brought thither from S. Francesco di Castelletto, when it was dismantled. His marble recumbent effigy is supported by

31

Staircase of Palazzo dell' Università, Genoa

three lions. Raised from a lowly position, he ruled with great
power and disinterestedness, and though the enmity of the
nobles caused his deposition in 1345, he was re-elected in
1356; after which the wisdom of his government and his
conciliatory power raised Genoa to the foremost position
amongst the Italian States. In 1363, while entertaining Peter
de Lusignan, King of Cyprus, in a banquet at Sturia, he was
poisoned by Malocello, a noble Genoese favourite of the king.
His house is still known and marked in a neighbouring alley.

         *   *   *

At the end of the [Turin Public] Gardens, where they melt
into the open hayfields – completely in the country, though
so close to the town – the grand old Palace of Il Valentino
rises from the river bank. It was built in the old French style
by a French princess, Christine, wife of Vittorio Amedeo I
and daughter of Henri IV and Marie de' Medici. Of rich red
stone, with high-pitched roofs, tall chimneys, and heavy
cornices, it resembles some of the best châteaux of the Loire,
and, with its richly verdant surroundings, forms a beautiful
subject for a picture. Altogether, though those who have not

Il Valentino, Turin

seen these gardens in spring may condemn Turin as an ugly featureless city, those who have enjoyed their freshness, especially in May, when the white and crimson chestnuts are all in bloom, will carry away the impression of scenes of perfect Italian loveliness.

Beyond S. Ambrogio and over all rises the brown mountain side, with blue mist in its rifts, crowned by the vast pile of the Sagro, half convent and half castle. A steep mountain way (donkeys may be obtained) winds up behind the curious old church, through rocks and fragments of chestnut forest. Near the summit, it passes the little village of S. Pietro, and then emerges upon a terrace on the top of the rocks, whence there is the most glorious view, into a wilderness of snowy mountain-ranges. The Sagro itself, a huge mass of building, rises in the foreground, at the top of an almost perpendicular precipice, where it was built as a penance in the tenth century, by a certain Hugo de Montboissier, on a spot where Bishop Amisone had already been directed to found an oratory, by fire which descended from heaven and marked out its site. The most conspicuous portion externally is the apse of the church, which has a Romanesque arcade. Great flights of steps form the approach to a round-headed door facing the precipice, whence a tremendous staircase, supported by a single colossal pillar, ascends to the monastery, the walls being partly formed by the rock itself, which projects in huge

33

masses through the masonry. At the top of the first staircase a beautiful round arch with marble pillars, very richly sculptured, opens upon a second ascent leading to the church, which is exceedingly curious, with many fragments of ancient sculpture, and a fine Gothic tomb of Guglielmo di Savoia, who was abbot here. A door on the left forms the entrance to a little platform overhanging the rock called Il Salto della Bella Alda, from an imprudent damsel, who, having leapt once from the top in safety under the protection of the Virgin, attempted to do it again, and perished in the attempt.

Il Sagro di S. Michele

Here is the entrance to the vaults filled with modern tombs, to which Carlo Alberto caused a number of the earlier members of the House of Savoy to be removed from the church of S. Giovanni at Turin. It is scarcely possible to imagine anything more beautiful than the views upon which the monastery looks down. It contains several pictures of the surrounding scenery, by Massimo d'Azeglio, who was, however, but a poor artist. Prince Eugene, who never married, was a titular abbot of S. Michele. There were formerly 300 Benedictine monks here, now the monastery is a centre for the Missionary Preachers under the direction of the Rettore Carlo Caccia.

Villar

It is possible to drive (but the road is very bad) to Villar, a village with a vine-shaded street, and a glorious background of mountain peaks.

*   *   *

Aosta occupies the site of the city which was built for the permanent subjection of the Salassi, and to which Augustus gave the name of Augusta Praetoria. It speedily rose to prosperity, and became the capital of the whole surrounding region. Pliny speaks of it as the extreme point of Italy towards the north. S. Anselm was born at Aosta, 1053.

The town is entered by a noble Triumphal Arch of

Arch of Augustus, Aosta

Augustus (Arco della Trinità). To the right are the remains of a small Roman bridge of one arch, and of a ruin, shown as the amphitheatre, but in reality the straight wall of a theatre.

Courmayeur

There is a terrace upon the roof of the inn at Courmayeur where one may spend hours in silent watches, when all the world has gone to sleep beneath. The Mont Chétif and the Mont de la Saxe form a gigantic portal not unworthy of the pile that lies beyond. For Mont Blanc resembles a vast cathedral; its countless spires are scattered over a mass like that of the Duomo at Milan, rising into one tower at the end. By night the glaciers glitter in the steady moon; domes, pinnacles, and buttresses stand clear of clouds. Needles of every height and most fantastic shapes rise from the central ridge, some solitary like sharp arrows shot against the sky, some clustering into sheaves. On every horn of snow and bank of grassy hill stars sparkle, rising, setting, rolling round through the long silent night. Moonlight simplifies and softens the landscape. Colours become scarcely distinguishable, and forms, deprived of half their detail, gain in majesty and size. The mountains seem greater far by night than day – higher heights and deeper depths, more snowy pyramids, more beetling crags, softer meadows, and darker pines. The whole valley is hushed, but for the torrent and chirping grasshopper, and the striking of the village clocks. The black tower and the houses of Courmayeur in the foreground gleam beneath the moon until she reaches the edge of the Cramont, and then sinks quietly away, once more to reappear among the pines, then finally to leave the valley dark beneath the shadow of the mountain's bulk. Meanwhile the heights of snow still glitter in the steady light: they, too, will soon be dark, until the dawn breaks, tingeing them with rose.

J. A. SYMONDS

At Milan

The great centre of interest at Milan must always be its glorious cathedral, a brick building, veneered with white marble. It was founded in 1387, by Gian-Galeazzo Visconti, on the site of a more ancient edifice, the original church on this site having been spoken of by S. Ambrose when writing to his sister Marcellina, as 'the great new basilica'.

Great variety of opinion exists as to the beauty of Milan Cathedral, and, as a whole, the general feeling will be, that the oftener you see it, the uglier it seems externally. But, as to the exquisite beauty and finish of its Gothic details all will agree, though, in order to appreciate these thoroughly, it will be necessary to mount to the roof, guarded by an army of statues, Wordsworth's

'aerial host
Of figures human and divine.'

37

The ascent is also well worth while on account of the noble view of the Alpine ranges to be obtained from thence.

The Cathedral of Milan has been wonderfully contrived to bury millions of money in ornaments which are never to be seen. Whole quarries of marble have been manufactured here into statues, relievos, niches, and notches; and high sculpture has been squandered on objects which vanish individually in the mass. Were two or three thousand of these statues removed, the rest would regain their due importance, and the fabric itself would become more intelligible.   FORSYTH

A more unlucky combination of different styles or a clumsier misuse of ill-appropriated details could scarcely be imagined. Yet no other church, perhaps in Europe, leaves the same impression of the marvellous upon the fancy. The splendour of its pure white marble, blushing with the rose of evening or of dawn, radiant in noonday sunlight, and fabulously fairy-like beneath the moon and stars; the multitudes of statues sharply cut against a clear, blue sky, and gazing at the Alps across that memorable tract of plain; the immense space and light-irradiated gloom of the interior; the deep tone of the bells above at a vast distance, and the gorgeous colours of the painted glass, contribute to a scenic effect unparalleled in Christendom.

                                                J. A. SYMONDS

No lover of art must leave Milan without making an excursion to the wonderful Certosa and the old city of Pavia. Carriages may generally be procured at the station. Ladies are now admitted to see everything here. The Certosa stands in the midst of the unvaried Lombard plain, whose marshy meadows, ever resounding from a chorus of frogs, produce several crops in the course of the year. Thick bands of willows and poplars, which follow the ditches and canals, shut out the view on every side. Here Gian-Galeazzo Visconti founded (September 8, 1396) the most magnificent monastery in the world, as an offering of atonement for the blood of his uncle and father-in-law Bernabo Visconti and his family, whom he had sent to be poisoned at the castle of Trezzo. Since the suppression of monasteries, only eight monks have been allowed to remain here, barely sufficient to take care of the monastic buildings, and to show them to visitors.

The convent gate is covered with fading frescoes by Luini.

Gate of the Certosa, Pavia

It forms the entrance to a large quadrangular court, on the opposite side of which rises the gorgeous western façade of the church, which is coated with marble, while the rest of the building is of brick. This façade, which bears an inscription dedicating it to 'Mary the Virgin – mother, daughter, and bride of God', is covered with delicate arabesques, and small bas-reliefs of scriptural subjects, often beautiful in themselves, but producing, in their general effect, more of richness than of grace.

Turning south from S. Michele [Pavia] we reach the picturesque covered bridge, built by Gian-Galeazzo over the Ticino. The bridge is of brick with stone quoins. A hundred little granite columns support the roof. The waters of the Ticinus are celebrated by the Latin poets for their clearness and beauty:

'Frondentibus humida ripis
Colla levat pulcher Ticinus.'

CLAUD. *De VI. Cons. Hon.* 194

At Pavia

Broletto, Como

Joining the Cathedral [of Como], the great sanctuary of the Church, is the chief building of the State, the Broletto (town hall) of 1215, built in courses of white, black, and red marble. It is vaulted throughout beneath with heavy octangular pillars.

A few years ago the little port of Como, crowded with boats and guarded by twin chapels, was most picturesque. This has now been filled up and turned into a commonplace piazza with a fountain, in honour of the experimental philosopher Volta, ob. 1826 -a native of the town.

Como (1866)

There is nothing to see in the village [of Locarno], but good walkers should not fail to ascend the hill behind to the Convent of La Madonna del Sasso, founded in 1487. The convent is not remarkable, but by scrambling round some of the little paths behind it, a point may be reached – well known to our water-colour artists – in which it combines with the cliffs and the deep wooded gorges in the foreground, and the mountains and still lake behind, in a manner which is truly enchanting.

La Madonna del Sasso, Locarno

It is not generally known that Locarno was one of the first places to join the Reformation in Italy. Its inhabitants were required to embrace the Romish faith or submit to banishment, and, as they preferred the latter, 200 families were driven from their homes, March 3, 1555, and forced through the ice-laden Alps, to take refuge in the Grisons. The papal nuncio had sent officers to seize the principal of Locarno, Barbara di Montalto, on a charge of blaspheming the mass, but she escaped by a secret door leading to the lake, while her pursuers were in the house.

41

Porch of Cremona Cathedral

The Cathedral [of Cremona] was begun in 1107, consecrated in 1190. The transepts were added 1342, the choir in 1479. The magnificent façade towards the piazza was begun in 1274, at which time the great porch and the rose window were built under Giacomo Porata da Cremona, but the other decorations of red Verona marble were not added till 1491. The statues and the great marble lions are by Sebastiano da Nani, 1560. The interior of the cathedral is greatly wanting in architectural splendour, and the effect of the lofty transepts is entirely destroyed by the low arches which separate them from the rest of the church. The building, however, makes up in colour for what it wants in form, and is so entirely covered with frescoes and pictures as to form a perfect gallery of Cremonese art. Lanzi considers it as a rival to the Sistine Chapel in its pictorial magnificence.

✻   ✻   ✻

I remember a city, more nobly placed even than Edinburgh, which, instead of the valley now filled by lines of railroad, has a broad and rushing river of blue water sweeping through the heart of it; which, for the dark and solitary rock which bears the castle, has an amphitheatre of cliffs crested with cypresses and olive; which, for the two masses of Arthur's Seat and the ranges of the Pentlands, has a chain of blue mountains higher than the haughtiest peaks of the Highlands; and which, for the

Verona, on the Adige

far-away Ben Lodi and Ben More, has the great central chain of the St. Gothard Alps; and yet as you go out of the gates, and walk in the suburban streets of that city – I mean Verona – the eye never seeks to rest on that external scenery, however gorgeous; it does not look for the gaps between the houses; it may for a few moments follow the broken line of the great Alpine battlements; but it is only when they form a background for other battlements, built by the hand of man. There is no necessity felt to dwell on the blue river or the burning hills. The heart and eye have enough to do in the streets of the city itself; they are contented there; nay, they some-times turn from the natural scenery, as if too savage and solitary, to dwell with a deeper interest on the palace walls that cast their shade upon the streets, and the crowd of towers that rise out of that shadow, into the depths of the sky. That is a city to be proud of indeed.

RUSKIN, *Lectures on Architecture and Painting*

✳   ✳   ✳

Vicenza is emphatically the city of Palladio, 1518–80, and owes all its characteristics to that great architect. Those who cannot admire Palladio will not care about Vicenza. But though many may quarrel with his details, there are few who will fail to acknowledge the perfection of proportions, and the wonderful way in which his windows, doors, entablatures, and columns are all related to, and all balance, one another.

The palaces have also a great charm from the wealth of verdure and bright flowers seen through their wide-opening porticoes, giving such an idea of space and air within the walls of the town.

The sights which must not be omitted in Vicenza are the Piazza dei Signori and Palazzo della Ragione; the pictures of

43

Vicenza, from Monte Berico

S. Stefano, S. Corona, and in the Pinacoteca; the Teatro Olimpico, and a general survey of the buildings of Palladio, ending in a visit to the Rotonda, and the ascent to Monte Berico.

The town is divided by the Corso, which ends at the Porta Castello. Here, from the windows of our inn, we may begin our study of Palladian architecture, by looking down upon the admirable, never-finished fragment of the Palazzo del Conte Porto al Castello, generally known as the Ca' del Diavolo.

One great charm of Vicenza is its vicinity to the beautiful Monte Berico, which no one should fail to ascend (about half a mile), to the Church and Convent of S. Maria del Monte, built to commemorate an appearance of the Virgin, in 1428, but much added to in 1688. The church is a Greek cross with a cupola. It contains a fine picture by Bart. Montagna, 1500 – the Madonna and saints bewailing the dead Christ. There is a delightful walk beyond the church, along the ridge of the hill, whence the view of Alps and plain and city is most beautiful.

✳   ✳   ✳

The centre of past life and present death in Mantua is the Piazza S. Pietro, where nearly all that was once most important in Mantova la Gloriosa stands grouped around a desolate

Piazza S. Pietro, Mantua

square. On the right (as we stand with our backs towards the town) is the vast Castello di Corte, the palace of the Gonzaga, into which several later palaces have in the lapse of centuries been incorporated. On the left are the Duomo, the Palazzo Castiglione, and the tall tower called Torre della Gabbia, with the iron cage hanging from it in which criminals used to be exposed for three hours on three successive days. Close to this is the Torre del Zuccaro, and behind soars the graceful dome of S. Andrea.

*   *   *

Arqua was the home of Petrarch, and his house stands on the hillside, with a beautiful view over the wooded plains.

Petrarch's House, Arqua

45

'Amidst the Euganean hills,' he wrote, 'not more than ten miles from Padua, I have built myself a small but pleasant dwelling, surrounded by an olive grove and a vineyard, which suffice for the wants of a modest and not numerous family.' The poet's dwelling is marked by a small brick loggia, and contains the chair in which he died, his inkstand, and his stuffed cat.

> 'Half-way up
> He built his house, whence as by stealth he caught,
> Among the hills, a glimpse of busy life
> That soothed, not stirred. – But knock, and enter in.
> This was his chamber. 'Tis as when he went;
> As if he now were in his orchard-grove.
> And this his closet. Here he sat and read.
> This was his chair; and in it, unobserved,
> Reading, or thinking of his absent friends,
> He passed away as in a quiet slumber.'
>
> ROGERS

Castle of Este

The Castle [of Este] has grand machicolations. It will be looked upon with interest as the fortress which gave a name to the House from which our own royal family are descended; indeed, most of the royal families of Europe originate with Alberto Azzo, Marquis of Este, himself descended from the

46

Adalbati, Margraves of Tuscany. His first wife, the Swabian Cunegunda, was mother of Welf (Guelf), Duke of Bavaria, from whose eldest son, Henry the Proud, the Dukes of Brunswick and the Kings of Hanover and England are descended. From Giulio, the second son of Welf, the Dukes of Modena and Ferrara descended. The grandmother of the late Duke (Francesco V) of Modena was Maria Beatrice d'Este. Este itself passed into the hands of the Carrara in 1294.

Bassano

Bassano (inn: S. Antonio, tolerable, but overrun with black beetles) is a fine old town with a covered bridge over the Brenta, and is overlooked by a fortress built by Ezzelino da Romano, and now containing the *parrocchia*.

Just within the bridge is the house, marked by a fresco of the Annunciation, of the famous family of Da Ponte – Jacopo (Bassano), born 1510; his father Francesco (Vecchio); and his three sons, Leandro, Francesco (Giovane), and Girolamo. The Museo Civico (open 9 till 1 p.m.), joining the principal church in the upper of the three piazzas, is filled with the works of the Da Ponte family, collected from the different churches and convents in the town.

There are symptoms of costume at Bassano. The women wear wide-awake hats, generally of black velvet, adorned with brilliant bunches of artificial flowers, and they have huge earrings and quantities of chains falling low round their necks. In church they put on handsome veils of black or white lace, which have a very pretty effect: in country places the process of veiling and unveiling takes place at the church doors.

At the end of the Piazzetta [in Venice], towards the lagoon, are two huge granite pillars, brought from one of the islands of the Archipelago in 1127. One is surmounted by the Lion of S. Mark.

Leone di S. Marco, Venice

The lion is made of many pieces held together by iron cramps. The pieces were made at different periods, the great number dating from the time when Doge Ziani erected the columns (1176). The eyeballs are probably of rock crystal. The wings are restoration, and were probably originally divided into feathers. The lion was gilded. 'It is looking into the distance, and its claws grasp the book: it seems to send a roar of defiance to the East.'

The Builder, July 19, 1884

The Church of S. Giuliano, – 'San Zulian' – a little behind S. Salvatore, was designed by Alessandro Vittoria and finished by Sansovino in the sixteenth century. Over the entrance is a very effective seated bronze statue of Tommaso da Ravenna by Sansovino.

48

ANNO MVNDI
VIDCC IIIII
NON S
OCTO
BRIS

IF SV CHRISTI
M D I IIII
V·R·BIS
M C
XXX
IIII

Over the Portal, S. Giuliano

Immediately beyond the Scuola di S. Rocco rises the great Gothic brick Church of S. Maria Gloriosa dei Frari. This church may be regarded as the Pantheon of Venice.

The tomb of Pietro Bernardo, 1558, by Alessandro Leopardi, is quite incomparable in design and delicacy of sculpture.

From the Bernardo Tomb at the Frari

49

Lily Capital, S. Marco

At the Ponte del Paradiso

Among 'pieces of detail' [opposite] Street finds the archway 'appropriately placed hard by the bridge called "del Paradiso" one of the most exquisite in the whole city'.

The main points to be noted are the characteristic flatness of the details and the line of dentil-moulding, which defines all the leading architectural features, originally invented for borders of incrustations at S. Mark's, and here, as everywhere in Venice, used for decoration afterwards. The incrusted circles of marble on each side of the figure give great life to the spandrel beneath the arch. The windows close by show us a late example of the not unfrequent use of the semicircular and ogee arches together in the same window.

STREET

There is a beautiful early Gothic gateway at the farther entrance of the Campo S. Zaccaria, with a relief, by the Massegne, of the Virgin between two saints.

Porta del Campo S. Zaccaria

The Gothic doorway in the low wall beyond the Church of S. Gregorio admits to the courtyard of the Abbazia, let in tenements, but indescribably picturesque, with its ancient central well of red marble, its dark arcades, supported by columns with richly sculptured capitals, and the masses of flowers which adorn its windows and parapets. Combined with the grand dome of S. Maria in the background, or with its open porch towards the glistening canal and old palaces on the opposite shore, it is a glorious subject for an artist.

In the Abbazia di S. Gregorio, Venice

Passing under the hideous iron bridge, we arrive at the steps of the Campo della Carità – the Field of Charity – belonging to the ancient convent of La Carità, which dates from the thirteenth century, and where the proud Alexander III took refuge in his exile. In the conventual church Doge Niccolo da Ponte was buried in 1585: part of his tomb by Scamozzi is now in the cloister of the Seminario Patriarchale. The conventual buildings are now occupied by the Accademia.

From the Campo della Carità

The Giardini Pubblici is one of the best points from which to watch the glorious Venetian sunset. Here is a description:

Le soleil était descendu derrière les monts Vicentins. De grandes nuées violettes traversaient le ciel au-dessus de Venise. La tour de Saint-Marc, les coupoles de Sainte-Marie, et cette pépinière de flèches et de minarets qui s'élève de tous les points de la ville, se dessinaient en aiguilles noires sur le ton étincelant de l'horizon. Le ciel arrivait, par une admirable dégradation de nuances, du rouge-cerise au bleu de smalt: et l'eau, calme et limpide comme une glace, recevait exactement le reflet de cette immense iridation. Au-dessous de Venise elle avait l'air d'un grand miroir de cuivre rouge. Jamais je n'avais vu Venise si belle et si féerique.

GEORGE SAND, *Lettres d'un Voyageur*

Venice from the Giardini

Chioggia (Hotel: Luna) occupies the whole of one of the larger islands. Its chief features are one immensely broad street, and one wide canal which perfectly blazes with colour – orange, yellow, crimson, and red – from the sails of its fishing-boats, which have the most extraordinary vanes at the top of their masts, wrought into the quaintest possible designs. When all these boats set forth and skim over the lagoon, it is like the flight of a swarm of butterflies. The people of Chioggia, too (Chiozzotti), retain all the finest characteristics of the old Venetian type, and painters still find their best models here.

Street of Chioggia

Cut off from the rest of the world by water, the life here is still the life of centuries ago, and Ariosto is even now [1900] read publicly in the evenings in the principal street, by a regular reader to a large and delighted audience.

Beautiful are the effects of sunset on the still lagoon, and still more perhaps the effects of moonlight, enjoyed by those who return in the evening from Chioggia.

*   *   *

The Cathedral [of Torcello] was rebuilt, evidently exactly in the form of an earlier church, in the beginning of the eleventh century by Orso the patriarch. The building contains many curious mosaics of the same date, and probably by the same artist as that at Murano. It has three parallel naves of ten bays, ending in apses. The stone shutters of the windows are almost unique. The columns dividing the principal nave from the aisles are of veined marble, with exquisitely wrought capitals, half Corinthian, half Byzantine. The holy water basin of the tenth century is very curious. The crypt is probably a remnant of a building of the seventh century. The choir is fenced off by a marble screen, 'the prototype of that at S. Mark's', and is adorned with sculptures of lions and peacocks, probably brought from Aquileja.

The cathedral was greatly injured and its exterior completely modernised during injudicious and hasty repairs under the Austrians, when the new roof was put on. The chancel is most remarkable, the seats rising in tiers with the semi-circular form of a theatre, and the episcopal throne of Orso in the centre raised above these seats, and approached by its own steep staircase.

Torcello

The Baptistery, or Church of S. Fosca, connected with the cathedral by a cloister, is a square church, with small projections on either side, and a deeper one on the east, where the high altar is raised above the relics of the virgin martyr Fosca, who suffered under Decius. Successive restorations have irretrievably injured the original character of the church.

On the site of the famous town of Augustus, Aquileja, which had more than 100,000 inhabitants, there are now only a few low cottages, and the one gigantic church which has risen upon the fragments of the early Christian cathedral – the crypt, baptistery and campanile – which alone were spared when every other building was so totally destroyed by Attila in 452, in revenge for the resistance he encountered here, that scarcely a stone remained perfect. The inhabitants had already fled with their treasures to Grado and to Torcello, and thus the destruction of Aquileja became the foundation of Venice.

Aquileja

The church – long the cathedral, now only a *parrochia* – has little ornament outside. It belongs mostly to the early part of the eleventh century, when the pillars which had been thrown down were again raised upon their foundations and newly enclosed. At the west end is a low portico, supported by heavy pillars, leading to the small solid church which was spared in the destruction of the ancient city.

Through this we enter the baptistery used for immersion in the time of Constantine, surrounded by six pillars, but now open to the air.

The great campanile stands in the cemetery quite detached from the church. It is well worth ascending for the sake of its wonderful view of the Alps, of Trieste and Miramar, and of the lagunes of Aquileja, which are something like those of Venice.

Piacenza is the best point from which to make the excursion to the famous Abbey of Bobbio (thirty-two Italian miles from Piacenza), founded by S. Columbano in 612, containing his tomb, and the place whence all the palimpsests known in the world have at some time or other emerged. It is a most fatiguing expedition. A carriage for three people costs 15 frs. to I Periti; when the road is finished it will probably cost 20 frs. to Bobbio.

Till 1876 there was no road beyond I Periti, where it was necessary to engage (5 frs.) the white mule of the *contadino Napoleone*, and to follow, as one best could, sometimes the stony bed of the Trebbia, sometimes the steep rocky path in

Bobbio

the hills overhanging it. The large town of Bobbio stands in the upper valley of the Trebbia, encircled by luxuriantly wooded hills, and has a long bridge of many arches of different forms and sizes. Deserted and neglected as Bobbio is now, it must always have special interest as the place where 'S. Columban lighted the flame of science and learning, which for a long time made it the torch of Northern Italy' [Montalembert] and whose school and library were perhaps the most celebrated of the Middle Ages.

*   *   *

The Church of S. Stefano, one of the most curious in Bologna, is said to have been built in imitation of the Church of the Holy Sepulchre, to which its only likeness consists in the union of a number of small churches under one roof. The chief portal (near which is an outside pulpit) leads into the Church of the Crocifisso of 1637. Hence some steps lead

S. Stefano, Bologna

down into the Chapel of the Beata Giuliana de' Banzi, who is buried there in a marble sarcophagus. The third church is S. Sepolcro, evidently an ancient baptistery (restored 1882), surrounded by marble columns, said to be taken from a temple of Isis, and rather like S. Vitale at Ravenna. Beneath the altar is the tomb which was intended to receive the body of S. Petronio, who is said to have rendered the water of the central well miraculous. The fourth church, SS. Pietro e Paolo, is said to have been the original cathedral of Bologna, founded by S. Faustinianus in 330.

The fifth church, which is in fact a small open cloister, called L'Atrio di Pilato, contains a mediaeval font removed from the baptistery, and a Crucifixion with SS. Jerome, Francis, and Mary Magdalen by Giacomo Francia, 1520. The sixth church, La Confessione, is a kind of crypt, in which the native martyrs Vitale and Agricola are buried. The seventh church, S. Trinità, contains a reliquary by Jacopo Rossetti, 1380, a figure of S. Ursula by Simone da Bologna, and some quaint pictures.

✻　　　✻　　　✻

Borgo S. Donino (inn: Croce Bianca) has a thirteenth-century cathedral, one of the richest and most beautiful of Lombard buildings. On the exterior are curious bas-reliefs. The porches are magnificent, and have different names. That called Taurus is decorated with bulls, that called Aries with rams, etc.

At Borgo S. Donino, Parma

The approach by road to Sestri is most beautiful. The mountains have grand and varied forms, the gaily painted churches and villages rise amid luxuriant olives and cypresses, and magnificent aloes fringe the rocks by the wayside.

Approach to Sestri

Sestri di Levante, the Roman Segesta (inns: Europa; Italia), is a charming spot, and quite worthy of a halt. There is a ruined chapel of black and white marble in a cove of the sea under the wooded promontory, and artists will find beautiful subjects in the ascent behind the town, looking towards Genoa.

✻   ✻   ✻

It is a drive of about eight miles (carriage 10 frs., a boat with one rower costs the same) along the western shore of the gulf to Porto Venere. The road passes above the bays of Cala di Mare, Fezzano, Panigaglia, Delle Grazie, Varignano, and La Castagna, and skirts a succession of villages, which have each their own little bay and shipping, and their old churches standing in groves of tall cypresses, or their ruined watch-towers. The driver will point out, not a hundred yards from the shore, a curious natural phenomenon in a spring of fresh water bubbling up out of the sea. At the mouth of the gulf is the island of Palmaria, three miles in circumference, famous in ancient times for its marble quarries, and now containing a fortress for the imprisonment of brigands. It has two attendant islets, Tino and Tinetto, on the former of which are the ruins of a convent.

Wonderfully picturesque is the little harbour of Porto Venere, where the tall, many-coloured houses come sheer

Gate of Porto Venere

down into the deep blue water. Here, by a strange eastern-looking gateway, one enters the narrow street, which ends on open rocks, at the extreme point of the promontory, where Byron wrote his *Corsair* upon the cliffs.

Lerici

A second excursion should be made to Lerici, at the southern point of the gulf. The road runs inland for some distance, but there is a noble view before arriving at the Pisan castle, with its high machicolated towers, fringed with golden lichen, and the town and harbour nestling beneath, while, across the still reaches of the gulf, glow the rocks of Porto Venere and Palmaria. Over the castle gate was the boastful patois inscription

> 'Scopa boca al Zenoese
> Crepacuore al Porto Venerese
> Streppa borsello al Lucchese'—
> ['A mouth-emptier for the Genoese,
> A heart-breaker for the Porto Venerese,
> A purse-stealer for the Lucchese']

carried off in triumph by the Genoese, who left lines of their own upon one of the towers.

*   *   *

The outline of the mountains, with their jagged precipices, becomes unspeakably grand after leaving Avenza, but the views reach a climax of poetic loveliness at Massa, where a noble castle crowns the rich olive-clad height above the town, while beyond it, the hills, dotted with convents and villas,

Massa Ducale

and radiant with vegetation, divide, to admit, like a fairy vision, the exquisitely delicate peaks of the marble mountains.

Massa Ducale (Albergo Quattro Nazioni, good) contains the immense palace of Elisa Bacciochi, Duchess of Massa Carrara, sister of Napoleon I. She pulled down the old cathedral to improve her view, and only one door of it remains, inserted in the modern building. The walks through the lanes and vineyards near Massa, watered by running streams, are exceedingly lovely.

*   *   *

Pisa is celebrated for its leaning tower, and for its mild winter air. But it strikes me as a hospital, where nothing flourishes but misery! The sky is grey, the earth is grey, the Arno is grey, and the quays along the rivers are crowded with beggars, young and old. . . . Happy they who have no

Pisa

necessity to live here on account of the mild winter air! Mild it is certainly, but mild as unsalted water-gruel. The city itself has a sickly, dying or dead appearance. It is, in fact, merely the corpse of the formerly powerful Pisa, the head of an independent republic.

FREDERIKA BREMER

At Pietra Santa

Pietra Santa (inn: Unione) is another exquisitely attractive point in this land of beauty. The old walled town has stood many sieges. Its perfectly mediaeval piazza contains a machicolated town hall of 1346, and two fine old Gothic churches, while behind rise the battlemented walls.

When the one beautiful group of buildings around the cathedral has been examined, the effect of what Landor calls

> ' – the towers
> Of Pisa, pining o'er her desert stream,'

will upon the *passing* traveller be only one of gloom and depression.

☆   ☆   ☆

Prato is a charming old thirteenth-century town on the banks of the torrent Bisenzio. The beautiful little cathedral, originally built in the form of a Roman basilica in the twelfth century, was enlarged c. 1320 under Giovanni

63

At Prato

Pisano, who added its cruciform shape. At one corner of the west front projects the pulpit of Donatello, of 1434, whence the 'Sacra Cintola' is exhibited – the girdle of the Virgin, said to have been brought back from Palestine in 1141 by Michele dei Dagomari.

From the Loggia de' Lanzi, Florence

To those who have not been much abroad, it will be sufficient amusement to sit for a time in this beautiful Loggia, if it is only for the sake of watching the variations of the fluctuating crowd in the Piazza below. The predominance of males is striking. Hundreds of men stand here for hours, as if they had nothing else to do, talking ceaselessly in deep Tuscan tones. Many, who are wrapped in long cloaks thrown over one shoulder and lined with green, look as if they had stepped out of the old pictures in the palace above.

Sitting here, we should meditate on the various strange phases of Florentine history of which this Piazza has been the scene.

Staircase of the Bargello

The Bargello is entered from the Via del Proconsolo. The courtyard is intensely picturesque and most rich and effective in colour; its staircase was built by Agnolo Gaddi. Near the well in the centre many noble Florentines have been beheaded, including (1530) Niccolò de' Lapi, the hero of Massimo d'Azeglio's novel. The beautiful upper Loggia is attributed to Orcagna: it was once divided into three cells, the farthest of which was for the condemned. The Loggia contains three bells, one of them from a church near Pisa, by one Bartolommeo, a popular decorative artisan under Frederick II.

S. George of Donatello, Or S. Michele

The exterior of Or S. Michele (which no one would take for a church) is adorned with windows of exquisite tracery and a noble series of statues erected by the different Guilds. They include Donatello's S. George of the Armourers, given by the Physicians and Apothecaries.

St. George is in complete armour, without sword or lance, bareheaded, and leaning on his shield, which displays the cross. The noble, tranquil, serious dignity of this figure admirably expresses the Christian warrior: it is so exactly the conception of Spenser that it immediately suggests his lines:

'Upon his shield the bloodie cross was scored,
For sovereign help which in his need he had.
Right faithful, true he was, in deed and word;
But of his cheers did seem too solemn sad;
Yet nothing did he dread, but ever was ydrad.'

JAMESON, Sacred Art, ii. 403

By the Via degli Speziali is, or was, the Mercato Vecchio
of which Pucci wrote:

'Le dignità di mercato son queste,
Ch' ha quattro chiese ne'suoi quattro canti
Ed ogni canto ha due vie manifeste.'

La Proprietà di Mercato Vecchio

This most interesting part of Florence was doomed to
destruction by its ignorant and short-sighted Municipality in
1889.

Il Mercato Vecchio

This, which was the 'Old Market' even in the eleventh
century, was the oldest part of Florence, intersected by
narrow alleys and full of quaint old houses. A cook-shop,
five hundred years old, in the Mercato itself, had interesting
majolica decorations. In the Via dei Vecchietti is, or was, the

place called Palazzo della Cavajola (of the Cabbagewoman) which belonged to the Vecchietti. Here Bernardo Vecchietto received Giovanni da Bologna, who made the charming bronze figure of the Devil, low down at the corner of the house, marking the site of a pulpit from which S. Pietro Martire exorcised the Evil One.

Bronze Devil, Mercato Vecchio

Here [in the Convent of S. Marco] are busts of Savonarola and his friend Girolamo Benivieni, imitations of old terracottas, by Girolamo Bastiniani (ob. 1868). Within are two small cells, which are of deep interest as having been occupied by Girolamo Savonarola, when Prior. His hair shirt, rosary, chair, and a fragment from the pile on which he was burnt are preserved here. In a desk, which is an imitation of his own, is a copy of his sermons, and – most interesting – his treatise against the 'Trial by Fire', and upon the desk is his wooden crucifix.

Savonarola embraced a monastic life in his twenty-second year, choosing the Dominican Order on account of his predilection for St. Thomas Aquinas. In 1490 he was elected Prior of S. Marco, and obtained leave to preach in the cathedral, finding his conventual church too small for the crowds who came to attend his sermons, for 'even in winter the

68

Bust of Savonarola, S. Marco

square in front of S. Marco was thronged for hours before the doors were opened, by disciples wishing for places', and 'tradesmen forbore to open their shops till the Prior's morning preaching was over'.

View from the Boboli Gardens

On Sunday, I went to the highest part of the Garden of Boboli, which commands a view of most of the city, and of the vale of Arno to the westward; where, as we had been visited by several rainy days, and now at last had a very fine one, the whole prospect was in its highest beauty. The mass of buildings, especially on the other side of the river, is sufficient to fill the eye, without perplexing the mind by vastness like that of London; and its name and history, its outline and large picturesque buildings, give it grandeur of a higher order than that of mere multitudinous extent. The hills that border the valley of the Arno are also very pleasing and striking to look upon; and the view of the rich plain, glimmering away into blue distance, covered with an endless web of villages and country-houses, is one of the most delightful images of human well-being I have ever seen.

JOHN STERLING, *Letters*

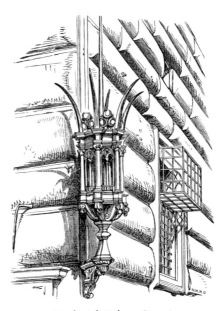

Fanale of the Palazzo Strozzi

Palazzo Strozzi was begun in 1489 for the merchant Filippo Strozzi from designs of Benedetto da Majano, which were continued by Il Cronaca. The palace is faced with rough-hewn stone which gives an appearance of extra finish to the details. At the corners are beautiful specimens by Caparrà, of the iron *fanale,* which were only allowed to the most distinguished citizens.

70

The interior of the palace is a handsome specimen of a noble Florentine residence. The best of the beautiful objects it contained have been dispersed, including the noble bust of Marietta Palla Strozzi by Desiderio da Settignano, and the portrait of the daughter of Roberto Strozzi ('La Puttina') painted by Titian and extolled by Aretino.

La Badia di Settimo

Four and a half miles from Florence is the old convent of La Badia di Settimo, now a villa. It has a fine old gateway, the front of which is decorated with a figure of Christ throned between two saints, one of the largest works of terracotta in Tuscany – built, not let into the wall. In Lent 1067, 8,000 persons collected here to witness the trial by fire, in which the Vallombrosan monk, Pietro Aldobrandini (afterwards canonised as S. Pietro Igneo), walked barefooted, unhurt, through a furnace, to prove an accusation of simony brought by S. Giovanni Gualberto against Pietro di Pavia, Bishop of Florence.

         ✳   ✳   ✳

Originally Vallombrosa bore the name of Acqua Bella. The convent owes its origin to the penitence of S. Giovanni Gualberto, who first lived here in a little hut. Within the first century of its existence his order possessed fifty abbeys. The habit of the Vallombrosans was light grey, but the late monks wore a black cloak and a large hat when abroad. The greatest severity was used towards the monks during the suppression of the religious orders, and scurrilous libels on the past history of Vallombrosa were purposely circulated. Yet the records of the Archivio show that in old times as many as 229,761 loaves of bread were distributed here to the poor in three years (1750–53), not inclusive of the hospitalities of the Foresteria, and in the same short space of time as many as 40,300 beech trees were planted on the neighbouring mountains by the monks.

Vallombrosa

The buildings of Vallombrosa are inferior in interest to those of other sanctuaries, and it owes its celebrity chiefly to its beautiful name and to the allusion of Milton. The church is handsome. The vast convent was chiefly built, as it now stands, by the Abbot Averardo Nicolini in 1637. While the monks remained, strangers were always hospitably received here. Since the suppression under the Sardinian Government, the place has lost many of its characteristic features, and the monastic buildings are used as a pension in the summer.

> 'Thick as autumnal leaves that strew the brooks
> In Vallombrosa, where the Etrurian shades,
> High over arch'd, imbower.'

> *Paradise Lost*, i. 303

In the Castle of Poppi

Crowning a hill about a mile to the right of the road is the town of Poppi, the old capital of the Casentino. Its castle, something like the Palazzo Vecchio at Florence on a small scale, was built by Arnolfo del Cambio in 1274, for Count Simone, grandson of Count Guido Guerra. It stands grandly at the end of the town, girdled by low towers. The staircase in its courtyard is wrongly said to have been copied from the Bargello at Florence. In the chapel are frescoes attributed to Spinello Aretino. A chamber is shown as that of 'la buona Gualdrada', mentioned by Dante (*Inf.*, xvi. 37), the beautiful daughter of Bellincione Berti, who declared to Otho IV, when he demanded her name, that she was the daughter of a man who would compel her to embrace him; upon which the maiden herself arose and said, 'No man living shall ever embrace me, unless he is my husband.'

✻　　　✻　　　✻

Here we must leave our carriage, and engage horses for the ascent to La Vernia, or Alvernia. The convent occupies the summit of a mountain, which was bestowed upon S. Francis, in 1224, by the knight Orlando da Chiusi, who was moved thereto by his preaching in the castle of Montefeltro. 'I have

73

a mountain,' he said, 'in Tuscany, a devout and solitary place, called Mount Alvernia, far from the haunts of men, well fitted for him who would do penance for his sins, or desires to lead a solitary life; this, if it please thee, I will freely give to thee and thy companions, for the welfare of my soul.' S. Francis gladly accepted, but the monks who first took possession of the rocky plateau, and built cells there with the branches of trees, had to have a guard of fifty armed men to protect them from the wild beasts.

The Gate of La Vernia

A rock-hewn path takes us to the arched gateway of the sanctuary, which has been greatly enlarged at many different periods since its foundation by S. Francis in 1213, but which to Roman Catholics will ever be one of the most sacred spots in the world, from its connection with the saint, who always passed two months here in retreat, and who is here believed to have received the stigmata, by which he was most especially likened to the great Master whose example he was always following.

Thrice in the week the monks kneel in the midnight around the marble slab where the stigmata were inflicted, and as the five lamps in memory of the five wounds of S. Francis are extinguished, they scourge themselves in the total darkness, and the clashing of the iron chains of their self-inflicted punishment mingles with the melancholy howl of the winds around the stone corridor. Twice in the twenty-four hours they join in a chanting procession down the long covered gallery on the mountain edge in honour of the stigmata.

Seeing the exquisite beauty of the bosco in spring, with its carpet of violets, primroses, daffodils, cyclamen, squills, saxifrage, and a thousand other flowers, we asked a monk if their loveliness was not a pleasure to him – 'Ma perchè? non mi sono mai confuso con la botanica,' was the answer.

Courtyard, La Vernia

The geography of Siena will be found exceedingly difficult from the starfish-like way in which its narrow promontories jut out, covered with houses and churches, and intersected by deep valleys. Inns: Grand' Albergo di Siena, Via Cavour, much the best, but expensive; Aquila Nera, Via Cavour, nearest the cathedral; Armi d' Inghilterra, nearest the station, a very poor Italian inn, but civil people – pension from 4 frs. to 5 frs. a day. Henry Hallam died in this house, and his picture hangs in the room.

The fountain – Fonte Branda – in the valley, enclosed in a Gothic building, has often been confused in guide-books with the Fonte Branda in the Casentino [the rich valley of the Upper Arno]. It was in the sandstone rocks behind the Siena fountain that the little S. Catherine made a hermitage for herself in a cave, in childish imitation of the hermits of the

Thebaïd. On the left of the steep street, Via Benincasa–(her family name), which ascends towards the town, rises distinguished by a sculptured gable, the House of S. Catherine of Siena, where she was born in 1347, and which was her principal residence during the thirty-two years of her life.

Inside they show the room she occupied, and the stone on which she placed her head to sleep; they keep her veil and staff and lantern and enamelled vinaigrette, the bag in which her alms were placed, the sackcloth that she wore beneath her dress, the crucifix from which she took the wounds of Christ. It is impossible to conceive, even after the lapse of several centuries, that any of these relics are fictitious. Every particular of her life was remembered and recorded with scrupulous attention by devoted followers.

J. A. SYMONDS

Descent upon Fonte Branda, Siena

The great church of S. Domenico is also much bound up with the story of S. Catherine, for here she took the vows of the third order of S. Dominic, and though she continued to reside in her father's house, and never lived in the convent as a professed nun, its church was the scene of many of her visions and ecstasies. The body of the church was built 1225–1465, the tower in 1340. Over the altar is one of the most interesting historical portraits in existence—S. Catherine by Andrea Vanni.

S. Domenico, Siena

No real lover of Italian art ought to miss a visit to Monte Oliveto, which is one of its greatest shrines. It is also only by taking a long drive like this that one can form an idea of the strangely peculiar country around Siena.

A steep ascent leads to Monte Oliveto through the barren desert of Accona. The volcanic clefts in the soil necessitate long détours, but the convent, with its mass of red buildings, is visible from a great distance, cresting the high hill of chalk and tufa, 'shaped like a chestnut leaf'. At about half a mile

Monte Oliveto

from the gates a narrow ridge is crossed, forming a sort of
natural bridge between two precipices. Here the scene
changes. Out of the desert we enter an oasis. The immense
depths below the monastic buildings are covered with rich
banks of wood: the road is fringed with cypresses embossed
upon the delicate distances of Monte Amiata, and with the
ancient olive trees which gave the place its name. Here again
the description of Aeneas Sylvius would suit the present time:

> Here are figs and almonds, and many kinds of pears and apples, and
> groves of cypresses in which you may take the air pleasantly in summer.
> Vineyards too, and walks in the shade of vine-leaves; and vegetable
> gardens, and pools for washing, and a perennial spring, and tanks, and
> wells; and groves of oak and juniper growing upon the very rock itself.
> And a number of walks, wide enough for two abreast, wind about or cut
> across the hill, with borders of vines, or rose-trees, or rosemary on either
> side. Pleasaunces delightful for the monks, more delightful still for those
> who, having seen, are free to go elsewhere.

S. Gimignano

S. Gimignano is a perfect sanctuary of mediaeval art, and one which no traveller should fail to visit. It may be seen in the day from Siena, or it may be taken on the way to Volterra, but artists will wish to give some time to the place itself. (The Albergo delle Due Piazze is clean and not unendurable to those who do not mind roughing it: very low charges.)

It is a pleasant drive of about seven miles from Poggibonsi – a small carriage (*legnetto*) costs 3 frs. Long before reaching S. Gimignano its strange group of thirteen tall mediaeval towers comes in sight, like a set of ninepins on the hilltop. Once, it was said, there were seventy-six of these *torroni*, all resulting from the ambition of every noble family to have a taller tower than its neighbour.

Tomb of Galla Placidia, Ravenna

An architectural feature of Ravenna will strike all visitors. It is that while all other campaniles in Italy are square, here they are almost all round. Still more may they be astonished to find all the 'Gothic' buildings entirely Roman.

From the front of this church [of S. Giovanni Battista] the Strada S. Crispino leads hence almost direct to the Church of SS. Nazaro and Celso, the famous Mausoleum of Galla Placidia. Outside it would not be recognised as a church, it is rather like a lowly outhouse of brick, the front not rising above the level of the wall in which it is engrafted. It is a Latin cross, 40 feet long and 33 feet broad, vaulted throughout, and with a cupola at the cross. In the centre is an ancient altar of oriental alabaster, formerly in S. Vitale, and referred to as existing in the sixth century. The three great sarcophagi are the only tombs of the Caesars, oriental or occidental, which remain in their original places. That in the chancel, of Greek marble, contained the body of the Empress Galla Placidia. Through a hole (now closed) in one of its sides the embalmed body of the Empress might once be seen (as Charlemagne at Aix-la-Chapelle), seated in her cypress wood chair and clad in her imperial robes, but in 1577 some boys set the robes on fire and the body was consumed.

Passing the Church of S. Maria Maggiore, we reach the magnificent Church of S. Vitale. This masterpiece of Byzantine architecture, externally a mass of rugged brick, was begun in 526, the year of the death of Theodoric, under the superintendence of the Archbishop S. Ecclesius and the *Julianus Argentarius,* under whom S. Apollinare in Classe was built. Its resemblance to the recently erected S. Sophia at Constantinople reveals its Eastern origin. It was erected in

At S. Vitale, Ravenna

honour of S. Vitale upon the place where he suffered martyrdom.

The lower walls of the church are coated with great slabs of Greek marble. The red marble with which the piers are inlaid is quite splendid. The carving of the capitals is of the most exquisite beauty; these blocks, sculptured in bas-relief, are a Byzantine feature, invented at Constantinople.

In the passage which leads from the basilica to the street towards S. Maria Maggiore is the Tomb of the Exarch Isaac, who died here in 641 (eighth Exarch of Ravenna). It is adorned with reliefs of Daniel in the Lions' Den, the Raising of Lazarus, and, on the front, the Adoration of the Magi, the last very curious – the Magi running as hard as they can with their gifts, their cloaks floating on the wind.

Tomb of the Exarch Isaac

The Strada Girotto leads into the Corso Garibaldi, on the opposite side of which is the grand Basilica of S. Apollinare Nuovo, built by Theodoric in 500, as the Arian Cathedral, under the name of 'S. Martino in Coelo Aureo'. When the Gothic kingdom fell, it was consecrated for Catholic worship by the Archbishop S. Agnellus. In the ninth century, when the relics of S. Apollinaris were transferred hither, it was called by his name. The twenty-four cipollino columns were brought from Constantinople, and have Byzantine

In S. Apollinare Nuovo, Ravenna

capitals. The roof is of wood. In the nave is the ancient pulpit, covered with curious sculpture. The last chapel on the left, which has an exquisitely wrought marble screen, sustained by four porphyry pillars, contains the sarcophagus which encloses the relics of S. Apollinaris, a bishop's throne of the tenth century, and a mosaic portrait of the Emperor Justinian, which once, with that of S. Agnellus, stood over the entrance of the church. The mosaics of the nave are, as a whole, more impressive than any other mosaics in the world.

Close to S. Apollinare, between it and the Strada di Porta Alberoni, is the fragment called the Palace of Theodoric, usually regarded as the only remnant of the famous palace of the Gothic kings, which was afterwards inhabited by the Exarchs and the Lombard sovereigns. The building, however, is early Romanesque – a high wall adorned with arches and columns. Against the lower storey stands a sarcophagus which an inscription, of 1564, states to have once contained the ashes of Theodoric, and to have stood on the top of his mausoleum. This is, however, very uncertain. The palace was ruined by Charlemagne, who, with the permission of Pope Adrian I, carried off its mosaics and other treasures for

Palace of Theodoric

the decoration of his palace at Ingelheim and his church at
Aix-la-Chapelle.

To the history-lover this wall will have a special interest
as part of the palace where the great Ostrogoth lived, where
'he used to amuse himself by cultivating an orchard with his
own hands', and where he died in 482.

About two miles beyond the gate called Porta Alberoni
(built 1793, in honour of Clement XII, as an approach to the
Port of Ravenna) is the desolate Church of S. Maria in Porto
Fuori, built at the end of the eleventh century, in consequence

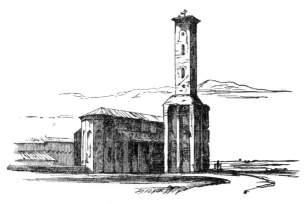

S. Maria in Porto Fuori

of a vow made at sea by one Pietro Onesti, called Il Peccatore. The name 'in Porto' is derived from the belief that the huge basement of the four-sided (here unusual!) campanile is that of the ancient Pharos, or lighthouse of the Port. The original pavement is now far below the surface, but Time has buried all the ancient buildings in Ravenna as in Rome. Many of the Princesses of the Polentani family were interred here in mediaeval times.

S. Apollinare in Classe

Such is the site of the old town of Classis. Not a vestige of the Roman city remains, not a dwelling or a ruined tower, nothing but the ancient church of St. Apollinare in Classe. Of all desolate buildings this is the most desolate. Not even the deserted grandeur of San Paolo beyond the walls of Rome can equal it. Its huge round campanile gazes at the sky, which here vaults only sea and plain – a perfect dome, star-spangled, like the roof of Galla Placidia's tomb. Ravenna lies low to west, the pine-wood, immeasurably the same, to east. There is nothing else to be seen except the spreading marsh, bounded by dim snowy Alps and purple Apennines, so very far away that the level rack of summer clouds seems more attainable and real. What sunsets and sunrises that tower must see; what glaring lurid after-glows in August, when the red light scowls upon the pestilential fen; what sheets of sullen vapour rolling over it in autumn; what breathless heats and rain-clouds big with thunder; what silences; what unimpeded blasts of winter winds!

J. A. SYMONDS

The vast church rises in the solemn silence of the Campagna, and its utter desolation gives it an indescribable interest, which is enhanced by its ancient associations, combined with the truth conveyed in its own inscription – 'Sanguis martyris semen fidei.'

84

Bridge of Rimini

At the lower end of the Corso is the five-arched Bridge of Augustus. Its arches are of the best Roman masonry. An imperfect inscription remains, commemorating the names and offices of Augustus and his stepsons.

✻   ✻   ✻

No one should leave Rimini without making an excursion to San Marino, about thirteen miles distant. It is a pleasant drive from Rimini through a fruitful plain. On crossing a rivulet about ten miles from Rimini, we enter the Republic. The malefactor who crosses the bridge over this stream cannot be pursued and is free for three days; after that, if he remains, he is given up to justice.

Borgo, the aristocratic and commercial centre of San Marino, stands just under the perpendicular cliffs upon which the upper town is built, and, in looking at their strange forms, we learn that the extraordinary mountains and rocks

S. Marino

introduced in the backgrounds of Raffaello, Perugino, Melozzo, and many other early painters, were taken from nature and were not nightmares.

From the castle on the highest point of the crags, there is a magnificent view over sea and land, and even the coast of Dalmatia is visible in the sunrise. The town contains about 1,000 inhabitants. Count Bartolommeo Borghesi, the well-known archaeologist and numismatist, resided here for some years. It is symbolic of the primitive state of affairs still existing in S. Marino, that the post never ascends the rock; when it arrives a great bell rings in Borgo, and anyone who wants his letters may come down and be present at the opening of the bag: if he fails to do so, he must wait till the next day.

✻   ✻   ✻

The whole scenery is the burnt landscape of Umbria, with the oddly-shaped valleys, the strange knobs and pinnacles of limestone rock, and the hill-set villages, of which the early painters made so much use. Quite unexpectedly, on crossing a mountain ledge, one comes in sight of S. Leo, a tremendous rock with utterly perpendicular sides, forming the most impregnable fortress. It is not strange that it was one of the three places selected by Dante to give an idea of the steepness of the Mount of Purgatory. The town is entered by a

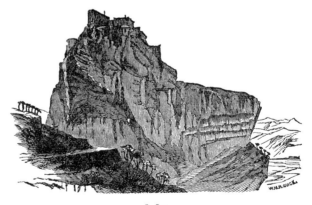

S. Leo

ledge in the rock and a tunnelled way. Its castle – 'La Rocca' – is a prison containing 300 prisoners. Its compartments, from their characteristics, are called L'Inferno and Il Paradiso. In the end room of the latter the famous Cagliostro died in 1795.

S. Leo was the most important fortress of the Dukes of Urbino, and was three times besieged while in their hands, the last time in 1516, when, in the reign of Duke Guidobaldo, it was captured by the Papal troops under Lorenzo de' Medici.

Arch of Trajan, Ancona

The view is charming over Ancona harbour, on the north side of which is the old mole, projecting from the foot of the hill called Monte Ciriaco, or Guasco, on which the town is built. The mole is adorned by the beautiful Triumphal Arch of Trajan, erected to his honour, A.D. 112, by his wife Plotina and his sister Marciana. Behind it, the cathedral of S. Ciriacus is seen crowning the hill.

   ✻   ✻   ✻

Loreto, 'the European Nazareth', next to Rome, is the most popular place of Christian pilgrimage in the world.

The Holy House of Nazareth, which witnessed the Annunciation, the Incarnation, and which was the home of the Holy Family after their return from Egypt, long continued an object of pilgrimage on its native site. The Empress Helena went to worship there, and erected a church over it, with the inscription – 'Haec est ara, in qua primo jactum est humanae salutis fundamentum.' S. Louis was among its later

Loreto, from the Recanati Road

pilgrims. But in the thirteenth century, when threatened with desecration by the Saracens, the angels are said to have taken it up (1291) and to have deposited it in a place of safety on the coast of Dalmatia, between Fiume and Tersato. Here it remained undisturbed for three years, but being again in danger, the angels again took it up, and bore it over the sea to this hill, up to that time called Villa di S. Maria, where they deposited it in 1295 in the garden of a devout widow called Laureta. The happy event was announced in a vision to S. Nicholas of Tolentino. The Holy House soon became an object of pilgrimage, and such offerings were made to the shrine as to excite the cupidity of the Saracens, against whom Sixtus V surrounded the place with walls in 1586, when Loreto became a city.

       ✳   ✳   ✳

The hill-set Macerata (inns – La Pace; Posta) is one of the most flourishing towns in this part of Italy. It has magnificent views of the sea and over the valley of the Potenza and Chienti. Its handsome palaces, for the most part built of brick, are only inhabited in summer.

The peasants seem here to observe a fixt uniform in dress, and orange is the prevailing colour. So constant are the women of this class to local costume, that the female head becomes a kind of geographical index. At

Macerata

Macerata they adhere to the ancient mode of plaiting and coiling the hair, which they transfix with long silver wires tipped at both ends with large nobs. At Recanati, they hang golden bells to their ear-rings, three or five to each chime, jingling like the *crotalia* of the Roman matrons. At Loreto, they adjust the handkerchief to their heads in the style of their Madonna. All the young men bind their hair in coloured nets, which is an old imitation of female attire, and, as such, was severely censured by Juvenal.

FORSYTH

✻   ✻   ✻

At Tolentino the Cathedral of S. Niccolò has considerable remains of old Gothic work, and an interesting cloister. The

Cloister of S. Niccolò di Tolentino

89

chapel of the saint contains his tomb, upon which the peasants throw money through a grating.

The great Augustinian saint, Nicholas of Tolentino, was born about 1239 at the little town of S. Angiolo in Pontano, near Tolentino. While very young he became an Augustinian monk. He was celebrated for his sermons, and was so distinguished by his austerities that it is said of him that 'he did not live, but *languished* through life'. His wonderful sanctity is said to have been foretold by the appearance of a star which rose from his birthplace at S. Angiolo and stood over Tolentino, and from this legend he is usually represented in art with a star upon his breast.

✳ ✳ ✳

Gubbio is a beautiful place, and singularly preserves its character of the Middle Ages. Close under the steep mountain-side, upon which its churches and palaces rise in terraces, it stands between the arid desolation of the mountains and the rich luxuriance of a fruitful and fertile plain. Cypresses break the gloom of its old brown houses, and, above them, high against the mountain-side, stands the beautiful Gothic Palazzo del Console, with the remains of the old Ducal Palace on a higher level still.

Close to the cathedral are the Casa dei Canonici, a mediaeval building, and the mutilated remains of the Ducal

Gubbio

90

Palace – 'La Corte' – built either by Francesco di Giorgio or Baccio Pontelli.

The mountain rises immediately behind the palace, and it stands so perched on its rocky edge that the paths which approach it must always have been precipitous, as they are still, but the workmanship of the doors and windows, which are all of marble, is most exquisite.

Ponte del Abbadia, Volci

A most desolate wind-stricken track leads from Montalto to Ponte del Abbadia, and, owing to the prevalence of malaria, the country is entirely uninhabited. This dismal prelude makes the transition all the more striking, when a path, turning down a hollow to the right, leads one into the beautiful ravine of the sparkling river Fiora, which forces its way through a rocky chasm overhung with a perfect wealth of ilex, arbutus, and bay, and is one of the most beautiful streams in Italy. The views near the bridge no one will omit, but there is a most lovely spot about a mile lower down the river called 'Il Pelago' (where an Etruscan bridge is said once to have existed), at which the river forms a deep rocky pool overhung by rocks and evergreens, which should also be visited, and, if possible, be painted.

Hence an ill-defined path leads along the edge of the cliffs to the Ponte del Abbadia, which presents one of the most glorious scenes in Italy. A gigantic bridge spans the river at a height of ninety-six feet, striding from one great orange-coloured cliff to another by a single mighty arch; while on the other side, close to the bridge, rises a most picturesque mediaeval castle with a tall square tower. From bridge and rocks alike hang stupendous masses of stalactites, often twenty feet in length, giving a most weird character to the scene, and formed by many centuries of dripping water, charged with tartaric matter. The whole view is filled with colour; the smoke of the large fires which the guards at the castle burn to keep off the malaria adds to the effect, and the utter desolation of the surrounding country only renders it more impressive.

Cervetri

Even from Palo station, the white walls of Cervetri may be discovered under the low-lying grey hills upon the right. The distance by the fields is about four miles, but by the high road it is nearly six.

(The best way of reaching the wonderful Cervetri is to walk from Palo. Sometimes it is possible to obtain a hired gig at Palo: seven francs is the proper price, to which the *vetturini* agree for going and returning, but the bargain must be made before leaving Palo. The sights of Cervetri must be visited in time to catch the evening train to Rome, for the only inn at Cervetri is so utterly wretched, it would be scarcely possible to pass the night there.)

The most conspicuous feature in distant views of the town is the ugly castle of Prince Ruspoli, who is Prince of Cervetri, and to whom most of the land in this neighbourhood belongs. The people all work in gangs, long lines of men and women in their bright costumes digging the land together. Most travellers who come upon them thus will be struck with the rude songs with which they accompany their work, one often leading, and the rest taking up the chorus in melancholy cadences.

As we pass the ruined church of 'La Madonna dei Canneti' in the reedy hollow, and ascend the hill of Cervetri, the walls built by its Orsini barons rise picturesquely along the crest of the hill, constructed with huge blocks of orange-coloured tufa taken from the Etruscan fortifications. They end in a mediaeval gateway.

Here we must enter the town to engage the *custode* of the tombs and insist upon his accompanying us, which, with true Italian love of 'far niente', he is not always very willing to do. Lights must also be taken. The ancient city, which was of oblong form, was nearly five miles in circuit, and filled the promontory, one small corner of which is occupied by the mediaeval town. Of the Etruscan city scarcely anything, except a few fragments of wall rising upon the tufa cliffs, can be discovered; but it is not so with the Necropolis.

Corneto

93

Turning down from the Monterozzi by the Grotta del Cardinale into the valley, the tourist should not fail to mount the opposite heights of Turchina or Piano di Civita, for, though there are no remains of the city except a few blocks of the masonry which formed the foundations of its walls, the view is most beautiful of the orange-coloured cliffs which are crowned by the towers of Corneto, and, beyond, of the wide expanse of blue sea with the beautiful headland of Monte Argentaro, its neighbouring islets of Giglio and Giannuti, and, in the distance, Elba, and even Monte Cristo.

Arco di Nostra Signora, Porto

The port of Trajan, still called Il Trajano, is now a basin of still blue water, surrounded by low underwood; along its sides the quays and warehouses by which it was once surrounded may still be traced. Near it, by the roadside close to the Villa Torlonia, is placed an inscription recording the cutting of the canals of Claudius in A.D. 49. Through the picturesque gateway, now called Arco di Nostra Signora, we reach the little group of buildings which is all that remains of the mediaeval town of Porto, consisting of the Bishop's Palace, and the little Cathedral of S. Rufina, with a tenth-century tower. The place was ruined at a very early period, owing to the Saracenic invasions, and though many Popes have made attempts to re-colonise it, they have always failed. As early as 1019 there were no inhabitants save a few guards in the tower of Porto, though it was the seat of a bishop, and though it has always continued to give a title to the subdean of the College of Cardinals.

Orvieto

From the valley itself rises, island-like, a mass of orange-coloured rock, crowned with the old walls and houses and churches of the town [of Orvieto], from the centre of which is uplifted the vast cathedral, with its delicate spray-like pinnacles, and its golden and jewelled front.

As we approach the town the difficulty of scaling its crags seems insurmountable. The road, though carried skilfully along each easy slope or ledge of quarried rock, still winds so much that nearly an hour is spent in the ascent. Those who can walk should take a footpath, and enter Orvieto by the mediaeval road, up which many a Pope, flying from rebellious subjects or foreign enemies, has hurried on his mule.

J. A. SYMONDS

Lake of Bolsena

The Lake of Bolsena is more than twenty-six miles round, and encircled by low hills. Two rocky islets break the expanse of water; on the larger, Bisentina, is an interesting church built by the Farnesi to commemorate the miraculous escape of S. Cristina from drowning; in the smaller island, Martana, may be seen the staircase which led to the bath where the Gothic Queen Amalasontha was strangled by her cousin Theodatus. The lake is full of fish, especially eels; Pope Martin IV died from eating too many of them.

The lake is surrounded with white rocks, and stored with fish and wild-fowl. The younger Pliny (*Ep.* xi. 95) celebrates two woody islands that floated on its waters; if a fable, how credulous the ancients! if a fact, how careless the moderns yet! since Pliny, the islands may have been fixed by new and gradual accessions.

GIBBON, V. 128

S. Flaviano, Montefiascone

Outside the Roman gate of Montefiascone is the principal sight of the place, the wonderful old Church of S. Flaviano, which dates from the eleventh century, but was restored by Urban IV in 1262.

The church is a most curious building, and highly picturesque outside, with a broad balconied loggia over a triple entrance. Within, it is one of the most remarkable churches in Italy; by no means subterranean, as it has been often described, nor has it even a crypt, but the triforium is of such breadth that it forms almost a second church, and contains a second high altar, and a bishop's throne, approached by staircases on either side of the high altar which covers the remains of S. Flaviano in the lower church. The pillars are most extraordinary, of enormous size, and with magnificent and very curious capitals sculptured with intricate patterns. Some of the side-chapels are almost in ruins. The whole building was once covered with frescoes, which are now only visible where a whitewash coating has been removed.

*   *   *

Civita Castellana is one of the most beautiful spots in this, the loveliest part of Italy. After a drive of several miles through luxuriant country, without any previous sign, the pastures suddenly open, and disclose a gulf in the tufa, a deep abyss of rock where the evergreen shrubs and honeysuckle fall in perfect cascades of luxuriance over the red and yellow tufa cliffs, stained here and there with dashes of black and brown, and perforated with Etruscan tombs of various sizes, reached by narrow pathways along the face of the precipice. In the misty depths the little river Treja wanders amid huge stones, and under the tall arches of a magnificent bridge of 1712, which crosses the ravine at a height of 120 feet. The opposite bank is crested by the old houses and churches of Civita; and in the hollow are some rustic watermills.

Gorge of Civita Castellana

97

The most remarkable remains of the ancient Falerium will be found near the Ponte Terrano, about a mile beyond the castle of Sangallo. The bridge crosses the ravine of the Rio Maggiore by a double arch; one pier is of rock, the other of Etruscan masonry. Wherever you turn around Civita Castellana, the ravine seems to pursue you, as if the earth were opening under your feet, so does it twist around the town. Each turn is a picture more beautiful than the last, and ever and again beyond the rocky avenues, Soracte, steeped in violet shadows, appears rising out of the tender green of the plain. The gorge has been compared to the famous Tajo of Ronda; it has no waterfalls, and the cliffs are not as high, but it is quite as full of colour and beauty. The traveller who merely spends a few hours in Civita knows nothing of it. In the early morning the hollows are filled with mist, while the sun lights up here and there a crag crested with ilex and over-hung with clematis and honeysuckle. Near the bridge a huge block of grey rock divides the valley and stands level at the top with the surrounding country, from which it must once have been riven – like an inaccessible island fortress in the midst of the ravine.

Convent of S. Silvestro, Summit of Soracte

On the supposed site of the ancient temple [of Apollo], 2,270 feet above the level of the sea, perched on the highest points of the perpendicular crags, its walls one with their precipices, now stands the monastery of S. Silvestro. It is a sublime position, removed from and above everything else. Hawks circle around its huge cliffs, and are the only sign of life. On a lower terrace are the church and hermitage of S. Antonio, ruined and deserted. To these solitudes came Constantine to seek for Sylvester the hermit, whom he found here in a cave and led away to raise to the Papal throne, walking before him as he rode upon his mule, as is re-presented in the ancient frescoes of the Quattro Incoronati at Rome.

Perugia

It is a long ascent from the station [at Perugia] to the grey city walls, which stand crowned with towers and churches at the top of a green hill covered with the utmost luxuriance of vegetation, 'as green as England and as bright as Italy alone'. Each turn of the way is beautiful, and most so on a market day, when it is almost blocked up with the herds of goats and oxen and flocks of sheep, attended by their gaily dressed herdsmen, who sing wild *stornelli* in deep Umbrian voices as they go.

The castle of Paul III has in its turn almost entirely perished under the existing government, and the frightful public offices which are such an eyesore in all distant views of the town have been erected on its site. Nevertheless all strangers will visit the open space which was once the platform of the fortress (now called Piazza Vittorio Emanuele) to enjoy the view, so unspeakably beautiful towards sunset, of the rich valley of the Tiber, with the churches of S. Domenico and S. Pietro crowning the nearer heights.

Lake of Thrasymene

Soon after leaving Camuccia, the railway begins to skirt the Lake of Thrasymene. Even when seen in this way it produces an impression different from that of all other lakes: it has a soft, still beauty especially its own. Upon the vast expanse of shallow pale-green waters, surrounded by low-lying hills, storms have scarcely any effect, and the birds which float over it, and the fishing-boats which skim across its surface, are reflected as in a mirror. At Passignano and Torricella, villages, chiefly occupied by fishermen, jut out into the water, but otherwise the reedy shore is perfectly desolate on this side, though, beyond the lake, convents and villages crown the hills which rise between us and the pale violet mountains beyond Montepulciano.

Artists will find charming subjects in the neighbourhood of Passignano, but they will do well to go thither for the day from Perugia; for the inn will scarcely be found endurable as to lodging, though it will supply a luncheon of eels or carp – 'Reina del Lago'.

*   *   *

The vast church of Santa Maria degli Angeli [in Assisi] is one of the great works of Vignola (1569). Half destroyed by earthquake in 1832, it was restored by Poletti, but the cupola remained intact. Enclosed in the midst of the bare

S. Maria degli Angeli, Assisi

interior, the little Chapel of the Porziuncula stands gem-like, its front blazing with colour. Over the entrance is a beautiful fresco by Overbeck (partly taken from Tiberio d'Assisi) of the Saviour and the Virgin throned in glory, sur-rounded by floating angels – being the vision of S. Francis, when he heard a voice saying, 'They shall take neither gold nor silver, nor money in their purses, nor shoes, nor staff: this is that which I seek.'

The Porziuncula, S. Maria degli Angeli

S. Chiara, Assisi

The Church of S. Chiara, close to the gate, striped in red and white, and with a lofty tower, is of great interest. The roadway passes beneath its enormous flying buttresses. The ceiling over the altar is decorated by thirteenth-century painters with figures of female saints (Agnes, Monica, Catherine, Chiara, Cecilia, and Lucia). In the right transept are injured frescoes by Giottino.

A flight of steps in front of the altar leads to a crypt, where you stand in darkness, and a nun, behind a grating in a lighted inner chapel, draws up a screen, and reveals the body of S. Chiara, the beloved friend and disciple of S. Francis, clad in the habit which she wore when living. The Reliquary contains the long flaxen tresses of the saint, cut off when she took the veil, her boxwood comb, and a skein of thread wound by her – also the (black) hair of S. Francis and his breviary.

✳   ✳   ✳

But the great sight of Assisi is the convent of S. Francesco, certainly one of the most remarkable buildings in Italy, beloved by artists now, and where, in past ages, as Rio says, 'all artists of renown have prostrated themselves in succession, and have left on the walls of the sanctuary the pious tribute of their pencil'.

Since the accession of the present Government the convent has been cruelly suppressed, only eight of the brethren being allowed to remain as chaplains, and these forbidden to wear the habit of the order. The grand religious services which were celebrated here some years ago no longer exist.

The building of the magnificent double Church of S. Francesco was begun in 1228, only two years after the death of S. Francis. The Lower Church was completed four years after, the Upper not till 1253. The body of S. Francis was removed hither in 1230. The architect was Jacopus, a German.

S. Francesco, Assisi

[Two miles from Assisi,] the Hermitage of S. Francesco delle Carcere stands in a cleft filled with luxuriant wood in the midst of the scorched and arid limestone rocks of Monte Subasio. A low gateway, with a fresco of the Virgin andChild between S. Francis and S. Chiara, is the entrance to a wood which is filled with wild flowers, and where nightingales sing abundantly. A knot of brown conventual buildings occupies the most picturesque position in the gorge, and encloses the cell whither S. Francis retreated as a young man to combat with his passions in perpetual solitude and penance. His stone bed is shown, and his wooden pillow, a fountain which burst forth in answer to his prayers, and the hollow by which the tormenting Devil escaped. In the dormitory is a large cross given by S. Bernardino. In the cell of S. Francis, now a chapel, is a miraculous crucifix which is said to have conversed with the nun Diomira 'di gran bonta e perfezione', and to have told her that it so loved two Franciscans (Fra

S. Francesco delle Carcere

Cristoforo of Perugia and another) that the whole world might be saved by their prayers. Not only this, but when Fra Silvestro dello Spedalicchio, overwhelmed by fatigue, fell asleep before it, it woke him with a cuff – 'un soavissimo schiaffo' – bidding him go and sleep in a more suitable place, i.e. his dormitory! Five other penitential cells remain in the wood, through the midst of which runs a stream which, when it threatened to destroy his hermitage, was stopped by the prayers of S. Francis. It is said that it now rages violently when any public calamity is at hand. In this wood, says one of his biographers, while S. Francis was singing the praises of God in French – to him the language of song – he was attacked by robbers, who, disappointed by his absolute poverty, for he possessed nothing but a hair shirt with a peasant's tunic over it, threw him into a ditch filled with snow.

✳   ✳   ✳

Few ravines are more full of beauty than the deep narrow gorge below Narni, broken here and there by masses of grey rock, elsewhere clothed with the richest green of ilex, cork,

Roman Bridge, Narni

phillyrea, arbutus, mastick and flowering heath. Just at the entrance of the glen, the famous Bridge of Augustus, which is considered to surpass all other bridges in boldness, carried the Via Flaminia over the ravine of the Nera, the Nar of classical times. Originally the bridge had three arches, of which one on the right bank is entire, and sixty feet in height. Martial alludes to it as the pride of the place in his days, when he accuses Narni, by its superior attractions, of taking away his neighbour Quintus Ovidius from his Nomentan farm. The bridge is now a grand ruin, ivy and shrubs garlanding its mighty parapets.

Close to the Roman ruin is an old mediaeval bridge guarded by a high gate tower, almost equally picturesque.

Mediaeval Bridge, Narni

Cathedral of Viterbo

The Cathedral (of S. Lorenzo) stands in a kind of close in the lower part of Viterbo, on a rising ground which was once occupied by a temple of Hercules, and which was called 'Castellum Herculis' as late as the thirteenth century. It is almost surrounded by different fragments of the half-demolished Palace where the Popes of the thirteenth century resided. In the great hall, which still exists, met the conclaves at which Urban IV (1261), Clement IV (1264), Gregory X (1271), John XXI (1276), Nicholas III (1277), and Martin IV (1277) were elected. The cardinals spent six months over the election of the last Pope, and made Charles of Anjou, who was then at Viterbo, so impatient that he took away the roof of their council chamber to force them to a decision, and they, in a kind of bravado, dated their letters of that time from 'the roofless palace'.

Adjoining it is another hall, still roofless, in which Pope John XXI (Pedro Juliani – a Portuguese) was killed by the fall of the ceiling in 1277. This room is supported by a single pillar, standing in the open space below, which projects through the floor so as to form a fountain.

John XXI was a man of letters, and even of science; he had published some mathematical treatises which excited the astonishment and therefore the suspicion of his age. He was a churchman of easy access, conversed freely with humbler men, if men of letters, and was therefore accused of lowering the dignity of the pontificate. He was perhaps hasty and un-guarded in his language, but he had a more inexpiable fault. He had no love for monks or friars; it was supposed that he meditated some severe coercive edicts on these brotherhoods. Hence his death was foreshown by gloomy prodigies, and held either to be a divine judgement, or a direct act of the Evil One. John XXI was contemplating with too great pride a noble chamber which he had built in the palace at Viterbo, and burst out into laughter; at that instant the avenging roof came down on his head. Two visions revealed to different holy men the Evil One hewing down the supports, and so overwhelming the reprobate pontiff. He was said by others to have been, at the moment of his death, in the act of writing a book full of the most deadly heresies, or practising the arts of magic.

MILMAN, *History of Latin Christianity*

Papal Palace, Viterbo

The wonderful position of Caprarola bursts at once upon those who emerge from the rocky way. Its grand, tremendous palace stands backed by chestnut woods, which fade into rocky hills, and it looks down from a high-terraced platform upon the little golden-roofed town beneath. In the buildings every line is noble, every architectural idea stupendous. Their design does not embrace only the palace itself, but is carried round the whole platform of the hillside in a series of build-ings, ending in a huge convent and church, built by Odoardo

107

Caprarola

Farnese. S. Carlo Borromeo, the great patron of idle alms-giving, came hither to see it when it was completed, and complained that so much money had not been given to the poor instead. 'I have let them have it all little by little,' said Alessandro Farnese, 'but I have made them earn it by the sweat of their brows.'

* * *

Tradition is wonderfully alive at Sutri. The house of Pontius Pilate is shown, and to the curse which he brought upon his own people it is said that the lawless nature is due for which the natives of Sutri have ever since been remarkable. At a corner of the principal street is the head of a beast, be it ass or sheep, which is believed always to be watching the hiding-place of great treasure with its stone eyes, but the authorities of the town, though they will not search for it

Sutri

themselves, have forbidden all other enterprise in that direction.

Some of the old palaces have beautifully wrought cressets still projecting from their walls. In a small piazza is a grand sarcophagus, adorned with winged griffins, as a fountain. The Cathedral has a lofty tower with trefoiled windows, and an *opus-Alexandrinum* pavement. It contains a portrait of Benedict VII, who was a native of Sutri, and of the canonised Dominican, Pius V, who was its bishop for five years.

Galera

Only a short time ago Galera had ninety inhabitants. Now it has none. There is no one to live in the houses, no one to pray in the church. Malaria reigns triumphant here, and keeps all human creatures at bay. Even the shepherd who comes down in the day to watch the goats who are scrambling about the broken walls, would pay with his life for passing the night here. It is a bewitched solitude, with the ghosts of the past in full possession. All is fast decaying: the town walls, some of which date from the eleventh century, are sliding over into thickets of brambles. Above them rise the remains of the fine old Orsini castle, from which there is an unspeakably desolate view, the effect of the scene being enhanced by the knowledge that the strength of Galera has fallen beneath no human foe, but that a more powerful and invincible enemy has been found in the mysterious 'scourge of the Campagna'. The only bright point about the ruins is the old washing-place of the town in the glen, where the waters of the Arrone, ever bright and sparkling, are drawn off into stone basins overhung with fern and creepers.

Bracciano

Beyond Galera, the road to Bracciano enters a more fertile district. Soon, upon the right, the beautiful Lake of Bracciano, twenty miles in circumference, and six miles across in its widest part, is seen sleeping in its still basin surrounded by green wooded hills. Then the huge Castle of the Odescalchi, built of black lava, and fringed by deeply machicolated towers, rises before us, crowning the yellow lichen-gilded roofs of the town. The steep ascent to the fortress can only be surmounted on muleback or on foot, and is cut out of the solid rock. On and in this rock the castle was built by the Orsini in the fifteenth century, just after their normal enemies, the Colonna, had destroyed a former fortress of theirs. So they were determined to make it strong enough. As we enter beneath the gateway surmounted by the arms of the Orsini, we see that the rock still forms the pavement, and reaches half-way up the walls around us. The rest of these grim walls is of black lava, plundered, it is said, from the paving-blocks of the Via Cassia. Gloomy passages, also cut out of the solid rocks, lead off into profundities suggestive of the most romantic adventures and escapes. One does not wonder that Sir Walter Scott was more anxious to see Bracciano than anything else in Italy, and set off thither almost immediately after his arrival in Rome.

*　　*　　*

Every artist will sketch the Castle of Ostia, and will remember as he works that Raffaelle sketched it long ago, and that, from his sketch, Giovanni da Udine painted it in the background of his grand fresco of the victory over the Saracens, in the Stanza of the Incendio del Borgo in the Vatican, for here the enemy, who had totally destroyed the ancient town in the fifth century, were as totally defeated in the reign of Leo IV (A.D. 847–56). Procopius in the sixth century wrote of Ostia as 'a city nearly overthrown'. The present town is but a fortified hamlet, built by Gregory IV, and originally called by him Gregoriopolis. Artists will all regret the destruction of the tall pine, so well known till lately in pictures of Ostia, which stood beside the tower till it died in 1870. On the battlements, masses of the blue-green wormwood wave in the wind.

Castle of Ostia

A bridge, decorated with the arms of the Chigi, takes us across the last arm of the Stagno, with a huge avenue of pines ending on a green lawn, in the midst of which stands the mysterious, desolate Chigi palace, occupying the site of the

Approach to Castel Fusano

beloved Laurentine villa of Pliny. No road, no path even, leads to its portal; but all around is green turf, and it looks like the house where the enchanted princess went to sleep with all her attendants for five hundred years, and where she must be asleep still. Round the house, at intervals, stand gigantic red vases, like Morgiana's oil-jars, filled with yuccas and aloes. Over the parapet wall stone figures look down, set there to scare away the Saracens, it is said, but for centuries they have seen nothing but a few stranger tourists or sportsmen, and the wains of beautiful meek-eyed oxen drawing timber from the forest. All beyond is vast expanse of wood, huge pines stretching out their immense green umbrellas over the lower trees; stupendous ilexes contorted by time into a thousand strange vagaries; bay trees bowed with age, and cork trees with lichen – patriarchs even in this patriarchal forest. And beneath these greater potentates such a wealth of beautiful shrubs as is almost indescribable.

*   *   *

Nothing can exceed the loveliness of the views from the road which leads from Tivoli by the chapel of S. Antonio to the Madonna di Quintiliolo. And the beauty is not confined to the views alone. Each turn of the winding road is a picture; deep ravines of solemn dark-green olives which waken into silver light as the wind shakes their leaves, – old convents and chapels buried in shady nooks on the mountain-side, – thickets of laurestinus, roses, genista, and jessamine, – banks of lilies and hyacinths, anemones and violets, – grand masses of grey rock, up which white-bearded goats are scrambling to nibble the myrtle and rosemary, and knocking down showers of the red tufa on their way; – and a road, with stone seats and parapets, twisting along the edge of the hill through a constant diorama of loveliness, and peopled by groups of peasants in their gay dresses returning from their work, singing in parts wild *canzonetti* which echo amid the silent hills, or by women washing at the wayside fountains, or returning with brazen *conche* poised upon their heads, like stately statues of water-goddesses wakened into life.

Tivoli

The pencil only can describe Tivoli; and though unlike other scenes, the beauty of which is generally exaggerated in pictures, no representation has done justice to it, it is yet impossible that some part of its peculiar charms should not be transferred upon the canvas. It almost seems as if Nature herself had turned painter when she formed this beautiful and perfect composition.

EATON, *Rome*

113

Licenza

A short distance beyond Vicovaro, a road to the left turns up the valley of Licenza. The road comes to an end on the margin of the clear brook Digentia, which is here sometimes swollen into a broad river by the winter rains. On the further side of the white stony bed it has made for itself rises Licenza, cresting a high hill and approached by a steep rocky path.

* * *

The old road to Ariccia winds through the hollow, amid rocks and trees, which, alas, have lately been pollarded. Still the glen must always be full of beauty, and is the constant summer resort of landscape painters.

L' Ariccia

L'Ariccia is now chiefly remarkable for the huge palace of the Chigi family, built by Bernini for Alexander VII. It is noble and imposing in its proportions, as it rises on huge buttresses from the depths of the ravine. In the interior are some interesting rooms hung with exceedingly curious stamped leather, and a chamber containing portraits of the twelve nieces of Alexander VII, who were so enchanted at the elevation of their uncle, that they all took the veil immediately to please him. Apartments are let here in the summer months, and are very delightful.

From Albano we had to go on foot for the short and beautiful remainder of the way through Ariccia. Reseda and golden cistus grew wild by the roadside; the thick, juicy olive trees cast a delicious shade. I caught a glimpse of the distant sea; and upon the mountain slopes by the wayside, where a cross stood, merry girls skipped dancing past us, yet never forgetting piously to kiss the holy cross. The lofty dome of the church of Ariccia I imagined to be that of S. Peter, which the angels had hung up in the blue air among the dark olive trees.

H. C. ANDERSEN, Improvisatore

Galleria di Sotto, Albano

It is a beautiful walk or drive back to Albano, through the Galleria di Sotto, shaded by huge ilexes which were planted by Urban VIII, or are even of older date. These gigantic trees, acquainted for centuries, often lean together against the walls as if in earnest conversation; often, faint from old age, are propped on stone pillars, supported by which they hang out towards the Campagna. At the end of the avenue we come upon Pompey's Tomb, beneath which are some of the *capanne* or shepherds' huts of reeds, described by Virgil. On the opposite side of the Via Appia stands the Villa Altieri, consecrated now to the Italian heart as having been the residence of the noble and self-devoted cardinal, who died a martyr to his self-sacrifice in the cholera of 1867.

Up this same Alban Mount, to the temple of Jupiter Latiaris, which was for Alba what the Capitol was for Rome, the dictators of Alba and Latium undoubtedly led their legions when they returned in triumph. This solemnity, in which the triumphant generals appeared in royal robes, was unquestionably derived from the period of the monarchy: not would the Latin commanders deem themselves inferior to the Romans, or bear themselves less proudly, when they were not subject to the imperium of the latter, or show less gratitude to the gods.

NIEBUHR, *History of Rome*, ii. 368

The top of the mount is a grassy platform, in the centre of which is a Passionist convent, built in 1788 by Cardinal York, who destroyed the ruins of the famous temple for the purpose. The only remains are some massive fragments of wall and the huge blocks of masonry which surrounds a grand old

Remains of the Temple of Jupiter Latiaris, Monte Cavo

wych-elm tree in front of the convent. The Latin *Feriae* had been always celebrated on the Alban Mount; and there Tarquin erected the temple of Jupiter Latiaris, probably with the idea of doing something popular, in using a site once consecrated to the protecting god of the Latin confederation:

'Et residens celsa Latiaris Jupiter Alba.'

LUCAN, *Phars.* i. 198

Piranesi says the temple was 240 feet long and 120 wide – the having the width half the length being according to Etruscan taste.

Nemi

The village of Nemi (far more worth visiting than Genzano) is beautifully situated on the edge of a steep cliff above the lake, and is surmounted by a fine old castle which, after passing through the hands of the Colonna, Borgia, Piccolomini, Cenci, Frangipani, and Braschi, is now the property of Prince Rospigliosi.

Nemi occupies the site of the ancient town of Nemus. Diana must have had a grove and temple here as well as at Ariccia. The fountain into which she is supposed to have changed the nymph Egeria after the death of Numa is pointed out on the way to Genzano.

From Civita Lavinia

Civita Lavinia is approached by a terrace commanding a grand view across the Pontine Marshes to the Circean mount. It stands on the edge of the promontory and is surrounded by dark walls of peperino, in many places apparently of great antiquity. At the western extremity is a building which Gell imagines may be the *cella* of the temple of Juno.

✻   ✻   ✻

Above the Villa Pallavicini [in Frascati] is the Villa Aldobrandini, standing grandly upon a succession of terraces, designed by Giacomo della Porta, and finished by Giovanni Fontana for Cardinal Pietro Aldobrandini, nephew of Clement VIII. The villa is adorned internally with frescoes by Il Cavaliere d'Arpino. Behind it a succession of waterfalls tumble through a glorious old ilex-grove, into a circle of fantastic statues. The scene may once have been ridiculous, but Nature has now made it most beautiful.

At the Villa Aldobrandini, or Belvidere, we were introduced to the most multifarious collection of monsters I ever hope to behold. Giants, centaurs, fauns, cyclops, wild beasts, and gods, blew, bellowed, and squeaked, without mercy or intermission; and horns, pan's-pipes, organs, and trumpets, set up their combined notes in such a dissonant chorus, that we were fain to fly before them; when the strains that suddenly burst forth from Apollo and the Nine Muses, who were in a place apart, compelled us to stop our ears, and face about again in the opposite direction.

Palazzo Aldobrandini, Frascati

When this horrible din was over, we were carried back to admire the now silent Apollo and the Muses, – a set of painted wooden dolls, seated on a little mossy Parnassus, in a summer-house, – a plaything we should have been almost ashamed to have made even for the amusement of children. All these creatures, in the mean time, were spouting out water. The lions and tigers, however, contrary to their usual habits, did nothing else; and the 'great globe itself', which Atlas was bearing on his shoulders, instead of 'the solid earth', proved a mere aqueous ball, and was overwhelmed in a second deluge.

EATON, *Rome*

S. Maria in Trivio, Velletri

Velletri is in many respects a much better centre for excursions than Albano, being situated on the railway itself, so that tourists are saved the long drive down to the station, which makes excursions from the latter town so fatiguing. Its streets are wide and clean, and the air healthy and invigorating.

Opposite the Palazzo Lancellotti rises the beautiful tall detached campanile of Santa Maria in Trivio, raised to commemorate the deliverance of the city from the plague in 1348.

View of Norma

Norba and Norma are five long miles from Cori, and can be reached only on foot or on muleback without making an immense détour. The path emerges on the steep of the mountain, and clambers along, with precipices above and below, amid the wildest scenery. All around are grey rocks, with short grass between, on which the flocks of goats pasture, whose shepherds, clad in goatskins, are the only human beings we meet here. Hawks swoop overhead. It is a vast view over what looks like a boundless plain, for all the undulations and sinuosities of the country are lost to us at this great height. At length Sermoneta comes in sight and then Norma. Then the ancient Norba rises on the right.

Leaving the citadel of Norba, and descending slightly on the other side, we soon reach the edge of the precipice towards the marshes, and here, through a jagged rift in the mountain-side, we look upon Norma, perched like an eagle's nest upon the top of tremendous precipices of bare rock.

Ninfa

Instead of returning the same way, it is best to descend from hence to the valley, clambering down through the broken rock and sliding shale, clinging to the myrtle and Judas bushes, into the depths where, nestling under the hill, is Ninfa, almost as entirely a ruin as Norba itself. It is an unspeakably quiet scene of sylvan beauty, and there is something unearthly about it which possesses and absorbs every sense. If fairies exist anywhere, surely Ninfa is their capital; Ninfa, where Flora holds her court, where the only inhabitants are the roses and lilies, and all the thousand flowers which grow so abundantly in the deserted streets, where honeysuckle and jessamine fling their garlands through the windows of every house, and where the very altars of the churches are thrones for the flame-coloured valerian. Outside the walls you would scarcely believe it was a town, so encrusted in verdure is every building, that the houses look like green mounds rising out of the plain. It is as if Nature had built the city for a perpetual Feast of Tabernacles. One tall tower stands near the entrance and watches its reflection in the still waters of a pool white with lilies and fringed with forget-me-not. By the roadside a crystal spring rises in great abundance in a little basin of ancient brickwork, and falls into the pool, where it turns a mill, and a little further on becomes a lake, on which Pliny mentions the floating islands in his time, which were called Saltuares, because they were said to move to the time of dancing feet. Ninfa can never be rebuilt. Even the shepherds cannot dare to pass the night there. Death, garlanded with flowers, is death still. No sound will ever be heard but the hum of the myriad insects which float amongst the flower-possessed streets and houses, the croaking of the green frogs and the rustling of the wind in the tall bulrushes.

Temple of Minerva, Cori

There are few places in the neighbourhood of Rome which have so many or such fine remains of antiquity as Cori. Behind the church is a small garden, where we find entire the beautiful Doric peristyle of the Temple of Minerva, generally known here as the Temple of Hercules. Eight columns still remain, four in the front. Here the figure of Minerva, which now stands under the Senators' palace on the Roman Capitol, was found.

✻   ✻   ✻

All those who visit Segni should turn at once to the right after entering the gate (there is a poor inn where a tolerable meal may be obtained), and make the circuit of the Pelasgic walls which give the place its chief interest. They are formed by masses of rock jammed into one another, and though of no great height, almost surround the existing town, and are among the most extensive in Italy. In some places they are most picturesque, especially where a tall cross crowns the huge pile of stones, and stands out against the vast expanse of distance, for you look across the great depths to billow upon billow of purple Hernican hills, and beyond these upon all the ranges of the Abruzzi – still, in April, covered with snow.

From the Walls of Segni

Cyclopean Gate of Alatri

You are beginning to wonder where Alatri can be, when you see its huge Cyclopean walls rising against the sky at the end of a valley upon the left, and forming a terrace fit for Titans to walk upon, an architectural Stonehenge. The modern road winds into the town by a gradual ascent. The ancient approach is the earliest instance of a *cordonnata,* a hillside broken by steps, such as the approach to the Roman Capitol. The streets are full of mediaeval houses, with Gothic windows and loggias; and the two ancient churches have each a fine rose-window in the west front. But towering high above the buildings of all later ages are the Cyclopean walls of the Pelasgic city, forming a quadrangle, and quite perfect, as if they were finished yesterday: for though the stones are fitted together without cement, each is like a mass of rock, and the arched form of their fitting adds to their firmness. One of the ancient gates remains under a single horizontal stone measuring eighteen feet by nine. The figure of the Pelasgic god Priapus is repeatedly sculptured on the walls, and it has long been a semi-religious custom for the inhabitants to go out *en masse* to mutilate it on Easter Monday.

✻   ✻   ✻

Anagni clings to terraces on the bare side of the Hernican hills, with the most splendid views in every direction. Its streets perfectly abound in quaint architectural fragments, griffins, lions, open loggias, outside staircases, trefoiled windows, and great arched doorways, and still remind one of the expression 'municipium ornatissimum', which Cicero, in his defence of Milo, applies to this town.

It is a very short distance up the hill to the cathedral (S. Maria), which is the most interesting mediaeval building in this part of Italy, except the convent of Subiaco. The see dates from A.D. 487. On the wall, above what was once the great south entrance, Boniface VIII sits aloft, in robes and tiara, in his throne of state. Over his head, blazoned in gold

Entrance to the Cathedral, Anagni

125

and mosaic, are the illustrious alliances of the Caetani before his time. The steps beneath this statue, which must have had a magnificient effect in the open space, as seen from the valley beneath, were destroyed thirty years ago by a certain Marchese (even his name seems to be forgotten), and the present entrance is by the north, where a quaint winding staircase leads into a dark gallery, lined with curious old frescoes and inscriptions, and so into the cathedral.

✳   ✳   ✳

Behind Palestrina the mountain rises abruptly, bare and arid, and the town itself stands very high. Still higher, on the last peak, stand the huge ruins of the fortress, rebuilt in 1332 by the famous Stephen Colonna.

Colonna Castle, Palestrina

In summer the stagnation of Palestrina is enlivened by the presence of the Barberini family, who live, not at the palace with the mosaic, but at another lower down in the town, quite in a feudal manner, and, as Prince and Princess of Palestrina, hold receptions in their garden, to which all the small gentry of the place are invited.

Six miles beyond Cavi, after passing a chapel beautifully situated near an old pine and some cypresses, Genazzano rises in a valley on the left about half a mile distant from the road. It contains the shrine of the Madonna di Buon Consiglio, who *flew* hither through the air from Albania.

Genazzano

The festa of the Madonna of Genazzano, on the 25th of April, is one of the most celebrated and the most frequented in this part of Italy. A figure-artist should never fail to see it, and the most sanguine expectations as to colour and costume cannot possibly be disappointed.

※   ※   ※

To obtain a general view of the convent of the Sacro Speco, it is necessary to follow the lower path which diverges just beyond Santa Scholastica. A succession of zig-zags along

Sacro Speco, Subiaco

Subiaco

the edge of the cliffs, amid savage scenery, leads into the gorge, which is closed in the far distance by the rock-built town of Jenne, the birthplace of Alexander IV and of the Abbot Lando. We cross the river by a bridge, whence a path-let, winding often by staircases up and down the rocks, allows one to see the whole building rising above the beauti-ful falls of the Anio. We emerge close to the ruins of a Nymphaeum belonging to Nero's Villa, and nothing can be more imposing than the view from hence up the gorge, with the great rock-cresting monastery on the other side, and all the wealth of rich verdure on the nearer steeps, which take the name of Monte Carpineto from the hornbeams with which they are covered. The little chapel above the Sacro Speco is that of S. Biagio (S. Blaise), who is invoked when-ever any catastrophe occurs in the valley. Here, once every year, mass is chanted by the monks of Santa Scholastica.

The town formerly professed the utmost devotion to the Papacy, and the waggon-load of its wild flowers was one of the most suggestive and attractive of the presents to Pius IX on his anniversary, sent by 'La sua divotissima Subiaco'; yet now the names of the streets are all changed, and we have the eternal 'Via Cavour, Via Venti Settembre, etc.'. Costumes still linger here, but are less striking than further in the mountains. The men all wear bunches of flowers in their hats on festas, the women wear *spadoni,* ending in a hand, an acorn, or a bunch of flowers in silver. Beyond the Albergo della Pernice, and the gate built in honour of Pius VI, is a curious old bridge with a gate-tower over the Anio. One of the best views of the town is just across this bridge.

✳   ✳   ✳

Leaving Monte Giove on the left, the road soon reaches a wilderness of deadly asphodel, and then traverses a forest till it enters Porto d'Anzio, passing, on the left, the deserted Villa of the Popes.

The foundation of Antium is referred to Anthias, son of Circe and Ulysses, and to Ascanius. It was one of the Latin cities which united against Rome before the Battle of Regillus, but was afterwards taken by the Volscians, under whom it rose to great power and wealth. Hither Coriolanus retired when banished from Rome; and here he is said to have died. During the latter days of the Republic, and under the Empire, Antium was most prosperous; and it became a favourite resort of the emperors. Here Augustus received the title of Pater Patriae, and here Caligula was born. Nero, who was also born at Antium, was greatly devoted to it, and constructed a magnificent port here. Antoninus Pius built an aqueduct for the town; and Septimius Severus added largely to the imperial palace. Cicero had a villa here, and amused himself by 'counting the waves'. The place declined with the Empire. It has been much injured of late years by the filling up of its port; which is quite useless now except for very small vessels.

Porto d'Anzio

The earliest mention of Sermoneta is in 1222, in a bull of Honorius III. In 1297 it was bought from the Annibaldeschi by Pietro Caëtani, Count of Caserta, nephew of Boniface VIII. In 1500 Alexander VI besieged and took the town, putting to death Monsignor Giacomo Caëtani, and Bernardino Caëtani, who was only aged seven. Till this time there were no titles in Italy, the great personages were only 'Seigneurs' of their own lands; but with the Spanish Borgias this was changed, and Alexander VI made his own son Duke of Sermoneta. In his time the prisons here were erected, and well filled. When Julius II came to the throne, he restored Sermoneta, with all their other confiscated possessions, to

Sermoneta

the Caëtani, and also bestowed upon them the title which his predecessors had attached to the property. The Caëtani retained their complete feudal rights; even the power of life and death, until the nineteenth century.

The Castle of Sermoneta is exceedingly imposing externally, and encloses a vast courtyard, but only a small part of the building is now habitable. There are one or two fine old chimney-pieces, but the parts of the building in best preservation are the Borgia prisons, which occupy an entire wing, one below another, beginning with well-lighted rooms, and ending in dismal dungeons. The little town was the birthplace of the painter Girolamo Siciolante.

Lake of Avernus

Near the Monte Nuovo the road to Baiae branches off to the left, and that to Cumae ascends a hill. Following the latter, we soon have a lovely view across the Lake of Avernus, 'pestilent Avernus', to the sea.

There is little in the hills around Avernus, dismally barren in winter, though radiant with vines in summer, to recall the feeling with which this lake, the especial lake of the poets, was formerly regarded. The 'Tartarean woods' have entirely disappeared, and the hills are now perfectly bare which are described by Pliny as inhabited by the Cimmerii, who lived in a city of caves like the existing gipsies at Granada, and are represented by Festus as a race of men dwelling in regions impervious both to the morning and evening sun, then shut out by the thick forests.

The pestilential and sulphureous vapours which rose in the hollow encouraged the ancient belief in its supernatural qualities, and led to the erection of temples upon the shores of the lake, in order to appease the infernal deities, to whose realms it was said to be the entrance. Here Ulysses is supposed to have descended to the shades.

Hannibal tried to make himself agreeable to the natives by sacrificing to the terrible deities of Avernus, whilst he was reconnoitring the fortifications of Puteoli. But superstition vanished when the sacred groves were destroyed, and a canal was cut by Augustus to admit first the waters of the Lucrine Lake, and then those of the sea, into the stagnant Avernus, that he might form a port, the Portus Julius – large enough to contain the whole Roman fleet at once.

Nero, the great desirer of the impossible, is said afterwards to have entertained the absurd idea of constructing a canal, navigable for ships, from the Tiber to Avernus, and thence to the Gulf of Baiae, and works for this purpose were actually begun. The communication between the lakes was again cut off when the eruption and earthquake of 1538 formed the Monte Nuovo, but some remains of the canal which connected them may still be discovered.

Arco Felice, Cumae

The Arco Felice is a noble brick arch, 64 feet in height, and pre-eminently picturesque. The ancient pavement remains belonging to the road from Puteoli to Cumae. The steep banks are full of tombs. Very near the arch was the monument of Tarquinius Superbus, which Petrarch saw and describes in his *Itinerary*. A little to the left, after passing the arch, is the entrance to the vaulted passage nearly half a mile long, which was constructed by Agrippa to make a direct communication between Cumae and Avernus. It is now called La Grotta della Pace, from a Spaniard, Pietro della Pace, who brought it again into notice in the sixteenth century.

The island of Capri, the ancient Capreae, is a huge lime-stone rock, a continuation of the mountain range which forms the southern boundary of the Bay of Naples. Legend says that it was once inhabited by a people called Teleboae, subject to a king called Telon. Augustus took possession of Capreae as part of the imperial domains, and repeatedly visited it. His stepson Tiberius (A.D. 27) established his permanent residence on the island, and spent the latter years of his life there, abandoning himself to the voluptuous excesses which gave him the name of Caprineus.

On landing at the Marina, a number of donkey women offer their services, and it will be well to accept them, for the ascent of about one mile to the village of Capri is very hot and tiring. On the left we pass the Church of S. Costanzo, a very curious building with apse, cupola, stone pulpit, and several ancient marble pillars and other fragments taken from the palaces of Tiberius.

The little town of Capri, overhung on one side by great purple rocks, occupies a terrace on the high ridge between the two rocky promontories of the island. Close above the piazza stands the many-domed ancient church, like a mosque, and so many of the houses – sometimes of dazzling whiteness, sometimes painted in gay colours – have their own little

At Capri

Capri

domes that the appearance is quite that of an oriental village, which is enhanced by the palm trees which flourish here and there. In the piazza is a tablet to Major Hamill, who is buried in the church. He fell under French bayonets, when the troops of Murat, landing at Orico, recaptured the island, which had been taken from the French two years and a half before (May 1806) by Sir Sidney Smith. Through a low wide arch in the piazza is the approach to the principal hotels, Quisisana being the favourite resort of the English, Pagano of the German colony. There is a tiny English chapel.

Forum of Pompeii

The Forum is one of the most striking points in Pompeii, and is one of those whence the purple destroying mountain is best seen, rising above the red and yellow ruins of the city. It was never completed, and its pedestals for statues were for the most part unoccupied when it was swallowed up. On its south side are buildings called the Tribunals, supposed to have belonged to the Law Courts. On the east, at the corner of the Strada dell'Abondanza, is the Chalchidicum, pro-bably an Exchange, which was built (as is shown by a still existing inscription over the side entrance) by the priestess Eumachia. Its court was once surrounded by fifty-four columns of Parian marble; in a niche is a copy of the statue of Eumachia now in the museum. Beyond this, facing the Forum, is the so-called Temple of Mercury with a richly sculptured altar. Next comes the Curia, a kind of town hall, in a very ruinous state; then the Pantheon, sometimes called the Temple of Augustus, from his statue which stood here between statues of Livia and Drusus, all now in the museum. The well-known picture of the meeting of Ulysses and Penelope and many others were found here.

Street of Tombs, Pompeii

In the suburb called Pagus Augustus Felix, we enter the Street of Tombs, and may notice the Villa of Diomed.

In the house of Diomed, in the subterranean vaults, a number of skeletons were discovered in one spot by the door, covered by a fine ashen dust that had evidently been wafted slowly through the apertures, until it had filled the whole space. There were jewels and coins, candelabra for unavailing light, and wine hardened in the amphorae for a prolongation of agonised life. The sand, consolidated by damps, had taken the forms of the skeletons as in a cast; and the traveller may yet see the impression of a female neck and bosom of young and round proportions. It seems to the inquirer as if the air had been gradually changed into a sulphureous vapour; the inmates of the vaults had rushed to the door, to find it closed and blocked up by the scoria without, and, in their attempts to force it, had been suffocated with the atmosphere.

In the garden was found a skeleton with a key in its bony hand, and near it a bag of coins. This is believed to have been the master of the house – the unfortunate Diomed, who had probably sought to escape by the garden, and been destroyed either by the vapours or some fragment of stone. Beside some silver vases lay another skeleton, probably of a slave.

E. BULWER LYTTON

＊　　　＊　　　＊

The Abbey of Cava is most striking in appearance, though

Abbey of Cava

its façade is an addition of 1796. About the year 1006, Alferius, a young nobleman of Salerno, of the family of the Pappa Carbone, was sent on a political mission to Otho III of Germany by Waimar III, Prince of Salerno. At the then newly founded monastery of S. Michel de Cluse near Susa he fell dangerously ill, and was nursed by S. Odillon of Cluny, who was halting at the monastery on his return to Rome. On his recovery, the near sight of death and the teaching of S. Odillon decided him to renounce the world entirely for the service of God, and after the fulfilment of his mission and his return to Salerno, he retired to a cave above the gorge of the Selano, which had already been inhabited by Luitius, a hermit-monk from Monte Cassino. Here so many disciples gathered around him that, in 1025, Waimar III and his son made a donation to the church of the cavern and domain of Cava, where the monastery was founded.

Not in variety of interest, but in grandeur, in picturesque grouping and outline, and above all in loveliness of colouring, this Amalfi Riviera far surpasses any part of that from Nice to Genoa. Nothing in picture or imagination can surpass the colour of the sea; it is not blue, it is not purple, it is not green, but it is all of these by turns, nay, all of these

Watch-tower near Amalfi

together, flashing into and flashing through one another, and passing in the
distance into an indescribable blended hue of all three – the reflexion of
the amethyst in the surface of the turquoise. The whole coast is a series of
deeply-indented bays and coves, separated by bold and varied rocky promontories, each crowned with its ruined mediaeval fort, quaintly machicolated. In the little bays are various towns and villages: Cetara, Maiori,
Minori, Atrani, curiously piled up, each against its rocky glen with quaint
arcades and towers, and bright-coloured walls and houses – each with its
tiny strip of white beach, and boats, and swarms of children in scant
clothing or in none, splashing in the bright water. And thus, through a
series of such scenes of marvellous beauty, is Amalfi approached.

DEAN ALFORD

Amalfi

Turning the corner of the rocky promontory, we come at
once upon Amalfi (Hotel Cappuccini, kept by the admirable
family of Vozzi, one of the most comfortable small hotels in
Italy; pension, 12 frs.: the *old* hotel is a picturesque house
upon the shore, but the Cappuccini Convent, perched high
amongst the rocks, is now for the second time fitted up as a
hotel under the same proprietors).

'Only man is vile' in this earthly paradise. Without having
suffered from it, no one can imagine the dreadful pest of
beggars which has grown up under the Sardinian government,

and which makes a long stay in the once enchanting Amalfi almost unendurable. Three-fifths of the able-bodied men, and every woman and child, beg. The greater part of the population now loiter idle all day long in the streets or on the beach, ready to pounce upon strangers, and 'Qual' co', Signo' resounds on every side, till the traveller, half maddened, is driven back to his hotel, or into the higher mountains. The only hope of future comfort is *never*, under any circumstances, to be tempted to give to a beggar; once give, and you are lost.

The Hotel Cappuccini is a charming old house with *tourelles*, hanging cupids, and a broad balcony in the centre of Amalfitan life. Close by is a wonderfully picturesque boathouse, a relic of the old republic, and the boats coming and going, the net-mending on the beach, and the number of people in the windows, are a perpetual amusement. The shore is a series of pictures, which come to a climax in the view looking back from Il Cieco, where the beach comes to an end. Here travellers who provide themselves with a key from Don Matteo Vozzi, the landlord of the Cappuccini, may have access to a cottage and garden above the sea, where they can enjoy the beauty undisturbed: it is the only quiet spot in Amalfi.

✻   ✻   ✻

Solmona (inn: Il Toscana, dirty and miserable; Casa di Signor Raffaelle, rough, but civil people). This is a perfectly mediaeval city, grandly situated on an isolated platform,

Solmona

crowned by many towers, and backed by snowy mountains. Being the birthplace of Ovid, the principal street is called Corso Ovidii, and is adorned with a poor statue of the poet, who was tenderly attached to his native place.

The Corso crosses a small square containing a Casa Communale of 1522, of marvellous beauty, adorned with statues of sainted popes and cardinals between its richly traceried windows. In one of these the pilasters, which imitate palm trees, rest upon lions, while the rose above is upheld by floating angels. The great piazza, where snow-mountains are seen on all sides above the houses, is one of the largest in Italy.

In the heights of Monte Murrone, about two miles from Solmona, is the Cell of Pietro Murrone, afterwards Pope Coelestine V, where he lived as a hermit from 1239 to 1294. Above the cave of the saint a two-storied hermitage has been built in later days, and is adorned with rude frescoes. It is

Hermitage of Pietro Murrone

approached by a pathlet so steep that it will excite feelings of pity for the archbishops and bishops who in a time of worse or no footpaths scrambled up to announce the strange election of the hermit Murrone to the Papacy, and to carry him off, more like a frightened wild beast than a human being, to his splendid coronation at Aquila. No transition has ever been more extraordinary.

*　　　*　　　*

In the town of S. Angelo a fine octagonal tower, built by Charles of Anjou, rises at the end of the street. Here, above a vast cave, once stood a temple of the demigod Calchas. Long after even its ruins had perished, a shepherd, in A.D. 491, was shooting at a wild bull upon the mountain, when his arrow suddenly flew back to him. Startled at the prodigy, he consulted Laurentius, Bishop of Sipontium, who repaired to the spot to pray, After three days S. Michael appeared, and gave

Descent to S. Michele, Monte S. Angelo

the bishop advice which led to a great victory over the Saracens at Sipontium, and afterwards to the appointment of the saint as generalissimo! S. Michael also showed Laurentius the long-lost cave and an altar miraculously prepared, where the bishop at once celebrated the first mass. The shrine became one of the richest in Italy.

Now a long, rugged flight of steps, partly rock-hewn, descended by the pilgrims upon their knees, winds under Gothic arches to the caverned church – the grotto of the vision. Most picturesque are its vast recesses – one used as a raised choir for the canons; another perpetually dripping with water, completely caverned, containing the magnificent high altar, surmounted by a poor statue of the archangel, absurdly attributed to Michelangelo. Behind is a well – Il Pizzilo – whence water, supposed to cure every disease, is distributed to the faithful in a tiny silver bucket. At the side stands a magnificent episcopal throne of the twelfth century, resting upon lions, and adorned with a relief of S. Michael and the Dragon. Everything here has an appearance of the most extreme age, and the effects of light upon the broken steps and craggy walls, and of the statues in the gloom, are intensely striking.

✻   ✻   ✻

Avezzano (inn, tolerable) is a very dull country town, with a fine old castle at one end of it, now belonging to the Barberina, but originally built by the Colonna.

Castle of Avezzano

Castel del Monte is octangular, with octagonal turrets at the angles. Both its stories are vaulted. The chambers are desolate, and the windows open to the sky; but the arched ceilings, marbled doorways and high sculptured chimney-pieces are still almost as perfect as when the great Frederick was living here in 1240: their details are Italian, super-imposed on a German design. Lear narrates the legend that Frederick, having appointed one of the best architects of the day to erect Castel del Monte, sent one of his courtiers to bring him a report of the work. The messenger set out, but lingered in Melfi under the attractions of a beautiful damsel, till he was summoned to return. Believing that the

Castel del Monte

Emperor would never have time to visit the castle, and unable to describe it, he denounced it as a total failure, both as to beauty and utility. The Emperor, enraged at the account he had received, despatched guards to Castel del Monte to bring the architect to his presence, but he destroyed himself and his whole family in his terror upon receiving the summons. Horrified by the news of this catastrophe, the Emperor himself hurried to Apulia, and finding his beautiful castle unfinished, and his best architect lost through the falsehood of his messenger, dragged the offender by the hair to the top of the highest tower, and hurled him with his own hand from the battlements.

Taranto

Taranto has been compared to a ship, the castle at its east end representing the stern, its great church the mast, the tower of Raimondo Orsini the bowsprit, and the bridge the cable. The bridge separates the outer harbour or Mare Grande from the inner harbour or Mare Piccolo, a quiet, dark-blue lake occupied by oyster-beds and shell-fisheries. Nets suspended to the arches catch an immense number of fish as they return to the open sea with the ebb of the tide. Like Bari, the town has an eastern aspect, with its narrow streets, high white houses, and flat roofs, and its miserable, filthy, scrofulous population, which has been confined in the narrow space occupied by the Acropolis of the Greek city since the eleventh century.

✻   ✻   ✻

Most glorious is the view from the platform in front of the church [of S. Gregorio, Messina] which overlooks the town, and the deep blue straits, up which S. Paul sailed in the

From S. Gregorio, Messina

Castor and Pollux, with the Faro on one side and on the other the noble rock of Scilla, behind which Aspromonte and the rest of the Italian mountains are bathed in the most delicate amethystine hues. When brown monks are leaning against the ancient balustrades, or women are resting their huge red and green water-jars upon the parapet, an artist could not possibly wish for a more exquisite composition.

Scilla was the scene of one of the most awful events of the earthquake of February 5, 1783. After the first shock almost the whole population took refuge from their falling houses upon the seashore. The aged Prince Ruffo of Scilla wished to have awaited the result before the crucifix in his chapel, but was persuaded to fly towards his great inland castle of La Melia. Finding the road blocked up by rocks which had been hurled from the mountains, he returned to the shore, and after joining fervently with his people in the service of Ave Maria, prepared to pass the night in a boat which was drawn up on the south of the promontory. But at 7.30 p.m. part of Monte Baci, the next headland, thundered into the sea. The roar of the waters was heard as the sea was driven upon the opposite shore of the Faro, then came a vast returning wave in which the prince and 4,000 people were swept away.

Scilla

145

Piazza of Taormina

Taormina consists of one long well-paved street and its adjuncts, following the windings of a mountain ledge. It presents a series of pictures which never become wearisome.

Here, winter and summer alike, old women sit like immovable sibyls in the doorways, spinning all the day long: otherwise, in the hot hours, the street is almost deserted, but in the early morning and evening it is alive with noise and

Theatre of Taormina

tumult, when all the bells are clanging, the children hurrying to school or benediction, and the flocks of goats clattering in from the country to be milked.

The Theatre itself is semicircular, and is 377 feet in diameter on the outside. Its perfection of structure was celebrated, as a voice upon the stage could penetrate to every part of the building when it was occupied by an audience of 40,000. The scena, with its three gates and its intervening niches for statues, is in wonderful preservation: the architecture is Corinthian. The exact date of the building is unknown, but, from its material being brick, it is probably a Roman work, erected upon the site of a Greek theatre, and in Greek form.

Gate of Mola

In ascending again to Tauromenium, a strange eyrie-like village, perched upon a rock on the right, will recall scenes in the backgrounds of Raffaelle and Perugino. It is Mola, and is reached by a winding path which ascends the hillside behind the Porta Messina. This is the only approach to the little rock-girt city, and it was by it that Dionysius climbed up in the winter of 394 B.C., and surprised the garrison. Near the summit, the path becomes a staircase, and ends in a gateway, guarding the narrow pass, and bearing the date of 1578. One may descend by the castle of Taormina.

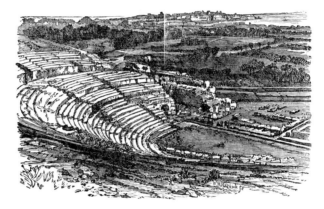

The Greek Theatre, Syracuse

The Greek Theatre, in its utter solitude, with its grey stones worn to the likeness of rocks and overgrown with flowers, and its exquisitely lovely view, is perhaps the most touching and attractive of all the Syracusan ruins. Readers of Tacitus will recall the excellent Pactus Thrasea, who was unjustly censured here by his detractors for opposing the proposal of Nero to allow the people of Syracuse a larger number of gladiators than was generally permitted. But it is difficult, indeed, to conjure up a picture of past scenes – of the theatre crowded, as must frequently have been the case, by 24,000 persons, and of Timoleon receiving here the thanks of the people for the restoration of their freedom. Now there is no sound but the murmur of a brook which once brought water to the busy city and turned the mills here, which gave the ruin its modern name of I Molini di Galerme.

Above the theatre is a Nymphaeum caverned in the rock, and close beside it on the left the entrance to the Petra-like Street of Tombs, cut out of the solid rock, and with walls entirely covered by monuments, some mere niches for urns, and others sepulchral porticoes overhung by masses of the beautiful caper plant (*Capparis spinosa*) which is the hyssop of Scripture. The marks of chariot wheels remain as deep ruts in the rocky way, and it is interesting to remember that down this hollow road the *lectica* of Timoleon must frequently have

Street of Tombs, Syracuse

been borne upon the shoulders of his fellow-citizens. Here also, especially, it will be felt how the Greeks and Romans, by thus bringing the dead amongst the living, must have kept their remembrance evergreen and modified the feeling of eternal separation.

✻   ✻   ✻

Euryalus is the key to Epipolae. Dionysius, when he enclosed Epipolae with walls, recognised the importance of the point, and fortified it with the castle which remains and is one of the most interesting Greek ruins extant.

J. A. SYMONDS

From the Walls of Epipolae

149

The view is most glorious from the summit of the broad ridge which gave the place its name, where, as in the verses of Theocritus, the goat still 'runs after cytizus' amongst the great stones fallen from the wall, which is built of huge blocks without cement. To the north is the winding bay, with the cities of Prioli and Agosta, and the rich plain sprinkled with liquorice-trees (*Glycyrrhica glabra*), while, above the mountains of Hybla, Etna soars with snowy altitudes into the pale blue sky, and is lost in mists beneath –

'the sea of cloud
That heaves its white and billowy vapours up
To moat the isle of ashes from the world.'

MATTHEW ARNOLD

To the south, we overlook, as in a map, the rich fever-bearing marshes of the Anapus; the hillsides once radiant with groves and temples, but now only covered with rocks and ruins, the abodes of lizards and serpents; the Great Harbour with Plemmyrium on one side, and on the other Ortygia, gleaming like a jewel on the face of the blue. One cannot wonder that the victorious Marcellus, as he stood upon these rock-built walls, 'was moved to tears, partly by joy over the feat he had accomplished, partly by the ancient glory of the city'.

*   *   *

Aci Castello is gloriously picturesque. A great orange rock is crowned by the ruins of an old castle. Far off, where the

Aci Castello

white village of Trezza sparkles, jewel-like, at the edge of the deep-blue sea, are the seven basaltic islets – I Faraglioni, called I Scogli de' Ciclopi – which, since the days of Pliny, have been said to be the rocks which Polyphemus hurled at Ulysses as he was putting out to sea. The foreground is covered with lava-rocks, twisted, contorted, black, but tinted by golden lichen, and their interstices are radiant with lovely flowers.

*   *   *

About a mile from its mouth, the muddy Anapus is joined by the clear Cyane. Now we leave the Anapus, and follow the smaller stream under its modern name of Pisma. Its narrow windings are often almost filled up by masses of

On the River Cyane

the beautiful papyrus (*Cyperus papyrus*), the plant of the Nile. It grows nowhere else in Europe, and was probably introduced from Egypt by the Syracusan rulers, in the time of their intimate relations with the Ptolemies.

Most exquisite in form and colour, the yellow plumes of the papyrus, supported by bright green stalks, feather in masses far overhead, and the boat soon seems lost in their thickets. Here and there only the papyrus gives place to beautiful oleanders or *palma Cristi*, or the river is chocked by floating tangles of ranunculus. The floating ranunculus becomes more solid, the papyrus grows more compactly, but the boatmen exclaim, 'Where we can go, we will go,' and, jumping into the shallows, force the boat on with their arms, or tow it from the bank. At length the river seems to disappear altogether in the glorious thickets of green, but the boatmen struggle through, and we suddenly find ourselves in a broad blue pool of transparent water, with open country towards the roseate mountains of Hybla.

Tomb of Theron, Girgenti

Just beyond the site of the [Girgenti] gate is the monument called the Tomb of Theron. Unfortunately it does not correspond with the description in Diodorus of the magnificent tomb of the despot, which the intervention of a thunderbolt saved from destruction when Hannibal ordered the tombs in the neighbourhood of the city to be destroyed, that he might use their materials in his earthworks.

Returning by the Porta Aurea, on the left is the entrance to the immense ruin of the Doric Temple of Jupiter, which was pseudo-peripteral. It measured 340 feet by 160, and is described by Diodorus as having been 120 feet in height, exclusive of the basement. Nothing now remains of the building but a confusion of prostrate fragments and pillars, and huge blocks of stone. But in the centre lies a gigantic statue in thirteen disjointed fragments. This figure, with

In the Temple of Jupiter, Girgenti

two others, stood erect till 1401, supporting a portion of the entablature, and Girgenti took them for her arms.

The gigantic head, which storm and overthrow have rendered shapeless, shows traces – Phrygian-fashion – of a *berretto* upon its curly hair. The arms are raised, as if to support a weight, as is the way with Caryatides. The figure, nearly thirty paluns long, is in the severe style of Egypt. It runs down to a point at the feet placed close together. It reminds one throughout of the huge statues of Memphis and Thebes. And here, stretched out, this brown and weird giant form appears like the god himself who has laid himself down in the midst of the ruin of his temple for a sleep of centuries, neither to be wakened by the earthquake and strife of elements nor by any sound from the history of a little human race.

GREGOROVIUS

Beyond the Temple of Jupiter, in the most lovely position, is the Temple of Castor and Pollux, the most picturesque

Temple of Castor and Pollux, Girgenti

ruin in Sicily. It had once six pillars in each front and thirteen at the sides, but only four columns are now erect, though many other lie prostrate amongst the palmetto and smilax. Exquisitely beautiful are the wild flowers here in spring – crocuses, lilies, asphodels, and a thousand others which Persephone would have lingered to gather, but they pass unheeded now: like Cometas in the fifth *Idyll* of Theocritus, the natives still prefer cultivated roses to the eglantine and anemones of the wayside.

La Cubola

Soon after leaving the Porta Nuova, we pass (left) the great Albergo de' Poveri, built by Orazio Fioretto, 1746. Then we reach the Cuba, a Saracenic palace erected by the Norman king, William II, in 1182. On the right of the road the gardener of the Cavaliere di Napoli will give admittance to an orange-garden, containing the small vaulted pavilion called La Cubola, which is the most perfect Saracenic remnant in Sicily, standing in what was once part of the gardens of La Cuba.

        *   *   *

S. Maria di Gesù, where a modern cemetery occupies the terraces near an ancient church, founded in 1429 by the Blessed Matteo di Girgenti, whose embalmed body reposes within, and, according to an inscription, has been known to rise and adore the host during mass.

From S. Maria di Gesù

In front of King Roger [in the Cathedral of Palermo] stands the sarcophagus (also brought from Cefalù) of his grandson, the great Frederick II, who died at Castel Fiorentino in Apulia, December 12, 1250: it was opened in 1342, when the body of the emperor was found, wrapped in the robe which had been given by the Saracens to the Emperor Otho IV when they wanted him to assist them. The epitaph is by his son Manfred.

Tomb of Frederick II, Palermo Cathedral

155

The magnificent cloister [of the Cathedral of Monreale],
169 feet square (*custode* 50 c.), is surrounded by pointed
arches, resting on coupled columns, often encrusted with
mosaics in varying patterns, with ever-varied classical capitals of marvellous beauty – 'all the religion, all the poetry of
their age, sculptured in stone'. At one corner is a fountain in
a little arcaded court, thoroughly Saracenic in character, 'as
of a monastic Alhambra'.

Cloisters, Monreale

Index

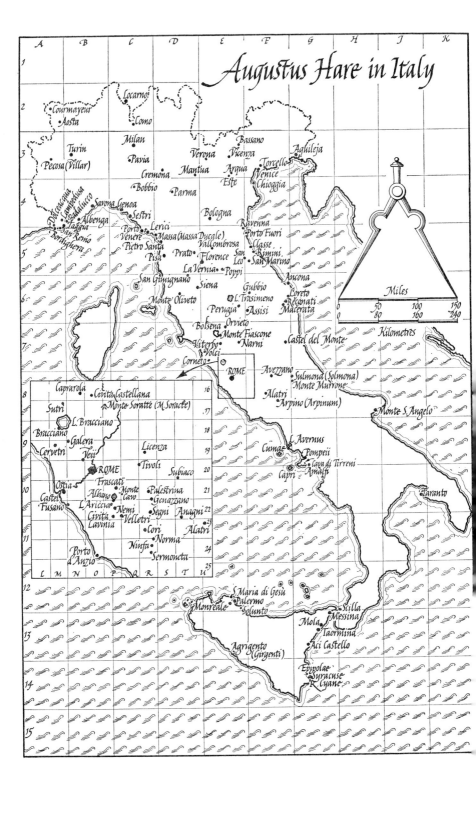

Index